PRAISE FOR DARITY WESLEY
Modern Day Oracle

You really are a Star, a shining star that shines brightly in my life. I thank you so much! *Stevie Rockliffe, Central Highlands of Tasmania*

I feel your words have truly helped me redirect my path and make me feel safer in this world. Thank you so much for your words and influence. You truly are a special being. You inspire more than you probably know. *T. Johnson*

It's amazing how often your spiritual posts have the answers or guidance that I am needing at that moment. You always take the high road and I love that about you. You have lived this way for a long time and your knowledge is incredible. I appreciate you very much. *Lynn Woehrle, Newman Lake, WA*

When I read the Oracle I get a feeling of safety, guidance and love! I always enjoy it and it always seems to fit what I'm *growing* through. Thank you so much for giving us this! *L. Monahan, La Mesa, CA*

Thank you for your years of wonderful advice and spiritual connection with the Universe, Darity. Your Oracles have been so valuable, and appreciated by those of us in your *ohana* all these years. I and many of my friends and family are faithful followers and appreciate your dedication in doing them. Mahalo nui loa! *Jo Byrne, Honolulu, Hawaii*

You just keep getting better and better. I really appreciate you and your consciousness. *Ed*

Your Oracles are powerful and life changing. I've been working with them for 2 years now and my life is completely transformed. Thank you, Darity, for your amazing work and extrao   idance. The Oracles have helped me tremendously! *M. Mo*

I have been reading, enjoying and supporting my thoughts with your Oracles for many years. I find them uplifting, positive and always right-thinking. I would miss these wise words if they were not presented with such love to me each day. J

I find your Oracles timely and thought provoking. I refer to you and your insightful topics as the 'way shower.' You are always on point. I look forward to the energy received when I read your insights. I love your Oracles! *Linda Strom Medvitz, Lakeside, CA*

I always SO enjoy your Oracles! It's part of my daily Spiritual practice. Truly, they are some of the most authentic, inspiring and insightful pieces simple and straight to the heart and soul. I often share them with family and friends to spread the Love. *J.B.*

Each day for the last two weeks especially, the Oracle has spoken directly to me. I have had major decisions to make, many things to let go of, the list goes on. And each Oracle helps me stay grounded. I love reading them! *Samantha*

Oh, I love receiving the Oracle! It's as if the Oracle is totally in harmony with whatever experiences are showing up. As if the Be-ing that I AM is dancing along a few steps, pausing, receiving the Oracle, joyfully and gleefully saying YES. *Sheila*

I'm at a stage in writing my book where the self-doubts are arising regularly (e.g. what the heck do you think you're doing, you have nothing new to say, your family is going to think you've completely fallen off the cliff, etc.) So the Oracle and reminders like this are a lifeline! In Love and Gratitude. *Susan Pearce, Fairhope, AL, author of OM-Less? An Irreverent Guide to Knowing Grace*

I want to let know how much you have impacted my life, way of thinking, integrity, and love. Your Oracles have really opened my eyes and heart and I am addicted. *T. J.*

How To Be
the REAL You

Darity Wesley

ORACLE™

Modern Day Oracle™ Wisdom Teaching Series
Book 2

Wesley, Darity
    How To Be the REAL You Darity Wesley – 1st edition 2018

Published by Lotus Wisdom Publishing

ISBN 978-0-9995425-2-1

Lotus Wisdom
Publishing

Dedicated to
the REAL you

BOOKS BY DARITY WESLEY

You Can Transform Your Life

You Can Transform Your Life ~ Go Deeper Workbook

How To Be the REAL You

How To Be the REAL You ~ Go Deeper Workbook

Featured Author

The Word Search Oracle: Yoga for the Brain

27 Flavors of Fulfillment

*Just when the caterpillar thought the world
was over, it became a butterfly!*
English Proverb

TABLE OF CONTENTS

Spiritual Maturity

Conclusion

FOREWORD

A little over a decade ago I was attending a *Women of Influence* networking event. It was at that time I met Darity Wesley for the first time, and my life was forever changed.

At this event, we went around the room to introduce ourselves and to share a little information about our businesses. I said my usual one minute enticement statement, to spark curiosity regarding the services my company offered. When it was Darity's turn, I remember her speaking about her law firm and her various businesses and publications. I was very impressed. It was her business entitled *Revive Your Spirit* that particularly caught my attention. My ears perked!

Darity went on to state that *Revive Your Spirit* was a business to connect people in the business world back to their Spirit. She said a few more statements about how we have disconnected from our authentic self. I was stunned! I quickly looked around the room to see if they were going to ask her to leave, hang her, throw daggers, I wasn't sure. This was during a time when in the corporate world, at least in the Fortune 500 company I worked with, you did not even mention the name *God* or anything about spirituality. Everything had to be kept underground. Not for Darity! She was fearless in sharing her truth with the world.

Once we had finished introducing ourselves, we were given time to do some networking. I could see three ladies walking over to where I was standing. I assumed they were coming to speak to me, as we were probably a good fit in business. I, on the other hand, *needed* to meet this Darity lady! So, I quickly turned and made my way over to Darity.

I introduced myself to her and we spoke for a few minutes. She was one of the most interesting people I had ever met. What made her different was that she was so assured in who she was. She stood firmly in herself and had no pretenses. She radiated confidence and wisdom. I was captivated by her and knew right away that I wanted to learn everything I could from her. We exchanged business cards and talked about setting up a future meeting.

A few weeks later we met again and continued meeting monthly, with each meeting lasting longer and longer. We had so much to talk about. And I had so much to learn!

In all my years of knowing her, she has always been so very authentically herself. Every word she speaks is aligned with who she *really* is and what she *truly* believes. I have learned so much from her and continue to work with and embody the teachings of "*Sage Darity.*"

Anyone who has had the pleasure to know Darity, or to have read any of her books or publications, knows that whatever situation we find ourselves in, we can turn to her wisdom and be inspired. We can feel her love and guidance supporting us, and cheering us on. Her wisdom always guides us back to our true, authentic self.

In *How To Be the REAL You*, Darity gives practical examples of how to be and move to the *true* embodiment of the REAL you. If you are wanting to learn more about yourself, or if you want to take your spiritual practices to a deeper more meaningful level, I highly recommend this book.

Dr. Wendy Kaveney is founder and director of operations of *SOUL: School of Universal Learning*, a newly formed charter high school located in North San Diego County, California. She is the author of <u>Me and My Senses</u>, a children's book, a columnist in *Women's Voices Magazine*, and is currently completing her second book entitled, <u>It's My Story and It is Sticking To Me!</u>™. She is the managing director of *Center of Love* groups internationally and is on the board of directors of *Conscious Humanity*.

It takes courage to grow up and become who you really are.
e.e. cummings

It is truly a courageous act to look, see and explore our deepest selves.

Wait! What???
Aren't I Already ME?

This Is About Discovering the REAL You

*Recognizing who you really are allows you to
shine forth in the world.*

When I bring up the subject of discovering who we really are, many folks say to me, *Aren't I already me?* Now that is a good question, don't you think?

My response is yes, of course you are you. However, the question is: Are you the REAL you? The authentic you? Are you the self-discovered you? Are you who you want to be? Are you who you *really* are or who you *think* you are?

To that you might reply, *I think I already am myself. So, how can I discover who I really am when I can't be anyone but me anyway?* That seems like another good question.

However, what if the *me, myself and I* that you *think* you are is not in fact the REAL you?

Well, that is indeed what this book is all about. It is about going on a journey of self-exploration and discovery so that we can begin to establish a stronger sense of who we really are. So that we can truly awaken to a greater, vaster and more authentic perspective of ourselves.

There Is Value in the Discovery

What do the words real, authentic and self-discovered mean in this context? More will be revealed along the way. However, at this point, I want us to take a moment and consider that there is *value* in the discovery. There is value in unlocking hidden doors within. Value in integrating practices to make positive change a habit. And there is value in bringing forth insights from both our internal personal worlds and from the external global world consciousness.

We Have All Been Conditioned ~ Say It Isn't So!

So, why don't we know who we really are? The answer is that we have all been conditioned.

Many of us are unaware, or haven't even thought about the fact, that we have all been conditioned to be who we are. Or, more accurately, that we have all been conditioned to be who we *think* we are. Really? Yes! We may have no knowledge of it happening at all or even understand that it is so. And even if we did, we may have no idea how to go about changing it if we wanted to.

For most of us, it's as if all beliefs about the way it is and the way things should be done were just fed into the computer of our mind and we accepted them – hook, line and sinker. Well, maybe sometimes we questioned them, but mostly we just accepted. This was done, usually, without any conscious thought on the part of the party doing the conditioning. They were just doing it the same way they were taught by their parents, or grandparents, or through books, by teachers, friends, colleagues or professors. Or simply from observing other people, even those seen in movies or on television. Or from feelings they had about the way things are or how things should be done. Or, more likely, all of the above!

I am not saying in any way that this is wrong or bad. In fact, I am not casting any judgment at all. We have all had this conditioning. It is part of being human. It's how we all learned to function as a human being and within a human society.

In fact, our conditioning began the moment we were born. Or, from a higher consciousness perspective, it became part of us at our first incarnation into a physical environment. Either way we choose to look at it, we have always been conditioned. It's a part of us.

Can this conditioning be changed?

Yes. Absolutely, yes!

Changing Our Conditioning

Even though this conditioning is part of us, it can be changed. In fact, if we want to be REAL, we must free ourselves from it. Not because it is wrong or bad, but because it is restricting us from being who we really are.

A lot of the time we know that we are not being REAL, not being genuine or not being honest with ourselves or others. Perhaps there have been times when we have wanted to say one thing, but have said another. Maybe even pretended to be something we are not, just to fit in or to be liked or to avoid being judged.

Imagine how it would feel to be free from that type of personal restriction. No phony baloney, no affectations, no pretentions.

Imagine how that type of personal freedom would *feel!* Free to be who we *really* are!

How do we free ourselves?

The first step is becoming aware.

Becoming Aware

If we want to change our conditioning, the first thing we need to do is become aware of it. We need to be able to really see it and recognize it within ourselves. This requires us to become more aware of what we are doing, what we are saying, what we are thinking. Once we are able to recognize our conditioning, we can begin to evaluate it and make changes to it if we want.

How do we know if we want to change it or not?

Once we become aware of a piece of our conditioning, we are in a position to choose. We can ask ourselves, *Is this piece worthwhile and something to keep?* Or *No, it does not serve me and I want to get rid of it, or change it up.* We will *feel* the answer. We will recognize that some of our conditioning is beneficial, and some of it is not helping us at all. Then we choose what is best for us. What feels the best. What feels REAL and true.

The main thing to realize is that we can become consciously aware of our conditioning. We can train ourselves to recognize it. And once we recognize it, and become conscious of it, then we have the opportunity to change it.

Keep in mind that in order to become aware of our conditioning, it helps to know and accept the premise that we really have been conditioned, and that we are the way we are because of it. As we begin to recognize our own conditioning, we are able to better understand why we have come to believe that this conditioning is who we are. We are able to discover and discern for ourselves what we really feel and what is really true.

That's what this book is all about. It is designed to help unlock the door of our conditioning and to help set us free. Free to be who we really are.

The Inward Journey Takes Courage

I spoke to a lot of people about this book topic while I was writing it, and was amazed at the many different reactions I received. Some of the people I spoke with were already at work exploring themselves and were very interested in the idea of becoming REAL. Some had not thought about self-discovery at all and were either curious or completely dismissive of the idea. And there was one person who said, with a laugh, *Well, I have always wanted to know who I am.*

The truth is, not everyone has the will nor the courage to take this inward journey. To look deep within, to explore and discover who they REALLY are.

Those who do take the journey understand that it requires a lot of dedication. It's not something that can be done quickly or easily. It's a process. One that is fun, meaningful and deeply worthwhile.

Self-Discovery Is an Adventure

In fact, the process of discovering and expressing the REAL you – the exploration – can be quite an exciting adventure! Things we may have never imagined come up, get cleared and we become freer. The light bulb goes off over our heads and we experience moments of *A-ha!* There is joy and revelation, discovery and passion. The dynamic, expansive, fun, difficult, heartbreaking, cathartic, soulful journey of self-discovery.

Knowing others is wisdom,
knowing yourself is enlightenment.
Lao Tzu

Self-Discovery

Knowing yourself is the beginning of all wisdom.
Aristotle

The desire to embark on the journey of self-discovery, and being able to recognize and acknowledge where we are in our life, is a benchmark. It's a beginning place. Even for those of us who have been on this journey for a long time, today is a beginning point. We take the time to acknowledge where we are in the process, and from there, we take our next step forward.

Clearing that internal voice that chatters on and on endlessly, the monkey mind, or at the very least learning how to manage it, supports us as we move into our self-discovery adventure. This adventure leads us to both personal and spiritual development and evolution. The journey of self-discovery also provides the energy to bring us happiness, harmony, peace, love and joy.

Know thyself.
An Ancient Greek Aphorism
Inscribed on the Temple of Apollo at Delphi

Throughout this book I will be sharing some stories, practices and vignettes from my personal life. I don't do this out of ego or the illusion that my personal life is so very entertaining, although I have found it to be so many times! I have included these stories to provide examples of the practices I am introducing, ideas for how to use them and how they have helped me.

Sometimes I might share my past struggle with a concept or idea, knowing that some of you might be struggling with or questioning it also. If my stories resonate, fabulous. If they don't, I'm sure we can all think of our own stories, our own examples, someone we know. Something we can relate to.

Our Experience Is Unique

The concepts and processes presented in this book will affect each of us in different ways. We will experience them in ways that are unique to us, individually. How they work for one may not be how they work for another. Even the way they work for us today may be different from the way they work for us tomorrow. They are each dynamic and changing. They change depending on what is going on and where we are on the journey.

My Personal Journey

I started my personal journey of self-discovery with a lot of deep and significant psychological work. I was 20 years old when I put myself into therapy. The reason I did it was because I felt that my life was a psychological casebook history: abandoned at an early age, alcoholic mother, two step-fathers, foster homes, early split from my biological brother/soul-mate, oldest of six children. Oh, so much fun! A lot to overcome.

Mostly, I put myself into therapy because I really wanted to find out what made me tick. I am really glad I did it, too, because it started me on a path of self-discovery which continues to this day. Over the years I sure have learned a lot. I have acquired a full toolbox of tools and practices and have integrated them to support my personal and spiritual development.

In the search for myself, I read a lot of self-help books. In fact, I have read so, so many books over the years that I plan to share some of my favorites with you along the way, just as I will share some of my personal experiences.

Self-Actualization: Reaching Our Full Potential

Early on in the process, I discovered the works of psychologist Dr. Abraham Maslow. His theories were based on the concept that every person has a strong desire to realize their full potential. His perspective supports the growth and development of our true and authentic self, which he calls *self-actualization.* He describes self-actualization as a part of human motivation, part of human evolution, part of growing and expanding our consciousness.

Dr. Maslow was truly a pioneer in his field. It was way back in the 1900s that Dr. Maslow wrote an article entitled *A Theory of Human Motivation* which appeared in <u>Psychological Review.</u> In this article, Dr. Maslow discussed a needs-based framework of human motivation. The basis of his theory is that human beings are motivated by unsatisfied needs and that certain needs have to be fulfilled before higher needs can be satisfied. He created a model for this which he called *The Hierarchy of Needs.*

The hierarchy is shaped like a pyramid. At the bottom level of the pyramid are basic physiological needs such as food, water, shelter and sleep. While at the top level we find the highest aspiration of self-actualization. According to Maslow, needs that are lower on the pyramid must become satisfied before one can move to the next level on the pyramid. Only then can one be in a position to seek the fulfillment of higher level needs.

According to Maslow, the highest level of self-actualization refers to becoming all that we are capable of becoming, the quest of reaching our full potential. This means growing and developing personally, psychologically and spiritually.

In order to achieve self-actualization, one must acquire new skills, take on new challenges and behave in such a way that will lead to the satisfaction and fulfillment of one's life goals. This made a lot of sense to me.

In order to focus on achieving self-actualization, however, all other human needs must already be satisfied. For example, I know there are instances where we may have wanted to spend more time on our personal development and spiritual growth. Yet, at the same time, we may not have been able to devote the energy needed to our spiritual and personal development because we were so focused on just trying to get by. Paying the bills, taking care of the kids or grandkids, keeping our career on track, keeping the car running, keeping food on the table. In essence, simply surviving and keeping the world at bay.

When our main focus is on survival, on simply taking care of our basic needs, these are the times when the monkey mind makes us feel anxious, afraid, scared, sad, hopeless, depressed and unable to move forward. It becomes a struggle to stay on top of depressing thoughts, or to get a handle on depression itself. (There is a whole chapter on the *monkey mind* coming up next!)

So, if this is what any of us feel sometimes, or all the time, know that this book is here to help. These are the keys that will help guide and unlock our understanding and, hopefully, inspire us in whatever it is we are wanting to do to evolve and grow.

The Work of Self-Discovery

Don't confuse knowing about yourself with knowing yourself ...
most people define themselves by the content of their lives ...
You are the inner space of consciousness.
Eckhart Tolle

One thing I quite often share with others is that self-discovery is not necessarily easy, yet it is not necessarily hard either. It is just the work. It is a process. It is an inside job and it is ours and ours alone to do. No one can do it for us.

The information presented in this book will serve as a helpful guide along the path of self-discovery. It is intended to bring forth an awareness of our own human conditioning and to offer tips, practices and tools that will help us to become more aware and more authentically ourselves.

Sacred Conversation Is Essential

As we venture deeper along the path of self-discovery, it will become more and more essential that we cultivate that sacred, on-going conversation between us and our Higher Self. When I refer to the Higher Self, I mean our own inner wisdom. In my belief system, that sacred conversation also includes our angels, guides and spirits, all of whom are here to support our personal development and growth at every level. In fact, that could be one of the main reasons to be reading this book right now – to assist and inspire that sacred communication to come forth in our lives, which is so vitally important.

It is time for all of us to bring forth new or different information from the deepest source of our own personal truth, from our own inner wisdom. This will support us immensely as we shift towards our very own self-actualization.

Journaling

Another helpful tool on the path of self-discovery is journaling. Taking the time to record our insights, feelings and experiences can enhance our self-knowledge and remind us of the important lessons we've learned. Our journal becomes a road map of our journey that we can return to again and again.

The print version of this book includes some blank lined pages, beginning on page 191, that can be used as your personal self-discovery journal to use along the way.

A Good First Step

The acknowledgement of where we are in life, where we are in the process of self-discovery, is a good first step. This provides a good foundation from which to begin to unlock the doors to the discovery of the REAL you.

Maslow's *Hierarchy of Needs* allows us to think about where we are in life in a structured way. It supports our quest for realizing our full potential, which is really about the development of our true and authentic self.

How we define our authentic selves changes over time. The ability to be the REAL you supports the possibility of energized moments of profound happiness and harmony. These make for a fulfilling life, for sure. It's an important first step!

What Is the Monkey Mind
and How Do We Tame It?

*The quieter you become
the more you are able to hear.*
Rumi

Quite often in conversation, I find myself referring to the *monkey mind*. I have used that term for a long time, yet I frequently come across a lot of people who are not familiar with it. Because I refer to it quite a bit throughout this book, I wanted to share a little background on what it means, just in case the term is not familiar.

As I researched where the term *monkey mind* came from, I was amazed to find that the concept arose over 2500 years ago with the Buddha. Here I was thinking it was some psychological term from the 1960s! Not so. The term has been around for a long, long time.

Let's take a look ...

Buddhism and the Monkey Mind

The use of the term *monkey mind* is attributed to Zen Buddhists who refer to the constant chatter of the mind as the mind of a monkey. The term was first used by Buddha to describe the human mind as a bunch of drunken monkeys jumping around, screeching, chattering and endlessly going on and on.

Buddha said that we all have monkey minds. He said that the mind is just like a monkey, swinging through a forest wilderness. It grabs one branch, then lets go of it, grabs another branch, lets go, grabs another, lets go and then grabs another and another. That sure does describe how the monkey mind works!

What Is the Monkey Mind?

When I'm asked what I mean by the monkey mind, I generally respond that it is the non-rational part of ourselves. However, it is really way more than that. Once we think about it and listen to ourselves, we can identify it. It really is the typical mind chatter: things to do, fears to fear, childhood dramas to relive, worries to have, judgments to make about ourselves and others, creating catastrophic what-if scenarios, or perhaps some coulda, shoulda, woulda fantasies.

The monkey mind, with its incessant voice in our head, has been programmed since birth. It has been heavily influenced by our own human conditioning and by the society we live in. Although it is a familiar voice in our head, it is not who we are.

The monkey mind is our inner critic. It is the voice that tells us that we can't do it. It tells us that we aren't good enough. It sits in judgment and tells us that we messed up or that we could have done better. It tells us that we are stupid, or useless, or unlovable, or even that we are pieces of doo doo sometimes, whatever! I am sure we all know what I am talking about here. The monkey mind creates false thoughts and insists on being heard.

The monkey mind is also a well-versed *outer* critic. It loves to sit in judgment of everyone and everything around us, offering an endless commentary of opinions as we go about our day.

Fifty Thousand Thoughts Each Day?!

I have heard that humans have around fifty thousand separate thoughts each day. Fifty thousand! And if we think about it, how many are basically about the same topic? Things like: *What will happen if I lose my job? What if my health declines? Do I have enough money? Is my partner unhappy in the relationship? Does so and so really like me?* Irrational fears which create feelings of anxiety, especially when we constantly pay attention to them. And they are not even real! This is our monkey mind talking!

Our monkey mind makes stuff up just to make us feel things that have nothing to do with truth or reality. Like Buddha said, it's a drunken monkey!

Need more proof?

The monkey mind dismisses, disregards and is highly suspicious of our intuition, our gut feelings.

Its commitment to self-pity can be endless.

It will encourage us to just give up and crawl back into bed.

Sound familiar?

It is amazing to me, when I look back, before learning how to tame my monkey mind, what I used to allow it to do to me. Oh yeah. Glad to be past that! I have to admit, though, it does still try to reassert itself occasionally. Luckily, with the arrows I now have in my quiver, I can shoot it down pretty quickly. Arrows we can all develop, which I will be presenting in this book.

That being said, we only want to shoot it down, we do not want to get rid of it. Oh no! It is very useful. I love my monkey mind. In our busy lives it's our monkey mind that keeps on top of things for us. It usually keeps us on time, on schedule, reminds us what needs to be done. It does have its practical applications.

Monkey Mind on the Loose!

The monkey mind is that part of us which is easily distracted and is incessantly moving. These are the settings where the monkey mind loves to run riot:

When we give our attention to too many things at once.

When we spend a lot of time rushing from one thing to the next.

When we spend time looking at what we have to do in the future instead of what we are currently doing.

When we spend time replaying events from the past.

That's when the monkey mind can go nuts on us. It's worrying about our trip next week, criticizing yesterday's performance at work, reminding us the car needs servicing, making up scenarios about what Jane said and how we should have responded ... on and on and on.

It takes a lot of self-control to shut it down. Yet, if we want to get anything done, or create anything new, or simply to have a moment of clarity, our challenge is to shut down the monkey mind for a while.

So, what can we do? Can we tame or train our monkey mind?

Yes, we can!

Taming the Monkey Mind

The untrained or untamed monkey mind can, especially when running free, cause us untold amounts of mental, emotional and spiritual suffering. This is one reason why meditation has become so popular. More and more people have become aware of the need to quiet the monkey mind. We feel exhausted from listening to that monkey mind ramble on, and of course it tells us to *relax, relax, there is so much more to do!* (Oh, yeah, thanks a lot!)

Most people are unaware that their monkey mind is causing their stress, depression and anxiety, among a host of other physical and emotional problems.

Even so, we do not want to get rid of the monkey mind, nor do we want to fight with it. We want to understand it, train it and live in harmony with it.

So, how do we do that?

Calming our minds is the first step.

Meditation

The Buddhists, as well as many others, work with the monkey mind through the use of quiet meditation. Focusing on the breath and noticing thoughts as they come and go, without engaging in them.

It does take some practice, especially if we have never tried it before. We don't need any formal type of meditation. We can just begin by following our breath in and out and being in the present moment. This is a great way to start.

Taking the time to sit still in quiet meditation, or even going for a walk in silence, can provide helpful insight into the way our monkey mind works. Simply notice thoughts as they come and go, without any engagement. This gives us an opportunity to notice and become more aware of our thoughts, more aware of our monkey mind.

Flattening the Button

When we take the time to really listen to what our monkey mind is saying, it responds. When we reason with it about the fears, anxieties and sadness it carries, we can point it in the direction of a more reasoned thought sequence. We have to continue the reasoned thought sequence when the subject pops up again. And I assure you, it will!

Once we stop the monkey mind enough times on a given subject, it will stop bringing it up. I call it *flattening the button*. That refers to the internal buttons that we all carry inside of us. Our sensitive spots. Other people, as well as our very own monkey mind, can push those buttons to get us to feel a particular feeling: anger, resentment, sadness, guilt, jealousy, insecurity, worthlessness, self-pity, anxiety, panic.

We each have our own monkey mind with our own conditioned feelings, our own familiar pattern of buttons that get pushed. The good news is, we are able to change them. We are able to flatten the buttons and not be triggered by them any longer, or at least, not as much. This enables us to tame our monkey mind, which is such an important tool. It allows us to find and create our true selves in a much easier fashion.

We have established that we need our monkey mind, just not in its excited, free-wheeling, drunken state. We need to keep a leash on it. What else can we do?

Here are some techniques that can help.

Techniques to Tame the Monkey Mind

Be in the Now

One thing most of us have in common is a monkey mind that likes to worry about the future. This is because the future is uncertain, no matter how much planning we do. None of us knows what is really coming. Things change minute by minute. This can often cause stress and anxiety.

We certainly have our visions, dreams, goals and intentions. If we are emotionally and spiritually mature, we know and understand that we can change them up if our lives suddenly change or shift direction. However, the monkey mind is not exactly the mature aspect of us. It is running wild on the loose and needs some adult supervision. It is quite often worried and anxious about what is going to happen next.

Approaching each day with anxiety or stress about what is going to happen, or what *might* happen, wreaks havoc on our bodies, as well as our beings. When we are apprehensive or worried about what is going to happen next, we lose the ability to be in the present moment. We might even miss what is happening right in front of us. In order to really appreciate and love the journey of life that we are taking, and to experience what is truly happening in the moment, we need to stay in the now.

Remember, the present moment is really all there is. When the monkey mind tries to get us to worry about the future, we can gently guide it to the realization that the present moment is all we are focusing on right now.

Taming the monkey mind challenges us to be in the here and now. We do not need to continue thinking and feeling old experiences that have nothing to do with now.

Freedom From Worry

Worrying is like paying a debt you don't owe.
Mark Twain

One of the greatest feelings we can have is to be *free* of worry. Worry is the monkey mind at work and all it does is feed our fears. If we think about it, worry does nothing at all to change the situation. According to Wayne Dyer, worry is one of those useless emotions that wastes our energy. I certainly believe that! It is a great concept to integrate and it's part and parcel of taming and training the monkey mind.

In my own practices, in order to integrate this concept and to tame my monkey mind, I created a process. Whenever I was getting off into worry about what *could* happen, I would say to myself, *What is the worst that can happen in this situation?* Then I would say to myself, *Can you handle it?* The answer was always *Yes.* I may not like it, however, I can handle it. I learned to focus on what is in front of me, the present moment, and not to create drama around something that was not happening. The monkey mind was assured that I could handle the worst, so everything in between was a piece of cake.

Have the Desire

Another important aspect of taming the monkey mind is to have the true desire to put an end to the monkey mind running wild. This is about making a conscious choice.

We are in control of our thoughts whether we are aware of it or not. Therefore, if we are not consciously controlling our thoughts, then who is? Yep, you've got it, the monkey mind! Therefore, in order to tame the monkey mind, and to be more in control of our thoughts, it is essential that we have the desire to do so. We have to consciously and wholeheartedly want it.

Listen and Analyze

Once the desire is in place, and when our monkey mind is in full swing, we can stop and listen to what it is saying. Then, once we've heard it, we can then take steps to reassure and help calm the monkey mind.

Step one is to listen. *What is it saying? Why is it upset? What set it off?*

Step two is to analyze.

Is it going on about something that needs to be done? Can it wait? If so, write it down. If not, and it's important, then do something about it.

Is it about something in the future? Is there anything we can do about it? Yes? Then write it down or do something about it. No? Then reassure the monkey mind and come up with a contingency plan. Write down the plan that helps.

Is it voicing resentment? Is it real? If so, create an action plan. Use your tools. Is forgiveness necessary? Gratitude? Any other needs? Sometimes the monkey mind just needs to be clued in that we have changed our perspective. It doesn't know until we tell it.

Is it just a complaint or judgment or non-stop commentary? If it isn't helpful in any way, just say, thank you for pointing that out, and then move along. Sometimes the monkey mind just wants to be heard.

Create a Distraction: Using Mantras

Another thing we can do is to interrupt the monkey mind with a distraction. In order to create the distraction, all we need to do is direct our thoughts to something else.

One way to do this is through the use of a mantra. Mantras are positive or neutral phrases that when used repetitively can help us with concentration. They create a distraction that liberates the mind from old thought patterns. When we recite a mantra, we pull our energy to one place by focusing on the statement, the word or the concept.

When we find the monkey mind has gone on its own journey, as it often does, stating a mantra over and over and over works to pull ourselves back to the present moment.

Here are some of my favorite mantras, which I use regularly:

All is Well

Be Here Now

Love and Trust

May Peace Prevail on Earth

Try these or come up with some of your own.

Another thing to do to interrupt the monkey mind is to look outside at nature. Look at and appreciate the trees, the clouds, the vehicles on the road, the rocks, the bridges, the blue sky, the birds, the flowers, whatever you see out there. No judgment, no thoughts about it, no good, bad or ugly, just observing. Direct the monkey mind to focus on gratitude for this beautiful planet we live on.

Creating a distraction can be anything that shifts our attention to something else. This is so that we can interrupt and distract the monkey mind.

Time to Yell *STOP!*

And then there are those times when the chattering monkey mind just won't quit. It may be time to really be adamant and yell for the monkey mind to stop. Sometimes more than once!

I do this a lot when my monkey mind is busy judging, whining, criticizing, complaining or assigning its own interpretation and meaning to what is happening in front of me. It goes on and on and on. And finally, I just yell, *STOP!*

I do this inside my head, of course. Although sometimes, when I am alone, I have been known to actually yell *STOP!* out loud. Boy, does that get the monkey mind to listen up quickly! I don't do it all the time. People might get concerned. Ha ha! But sometimes yelling *STOP!* is the only thing that works. And it does work!

Then, once I've yelled *STOP!* and my monkey mind gets quiet, I move into a state of compassion and love for myself, for others and for my dear monkey mind.

Turn Down the Volume

Essentially, taming the monkey mind is all about turning down the volume. As we turn down the volume of the monkey mind, we will find our energy levels will change. We will become calmer people.

The monkey mind tends to be reactive and impulsive, to lash out abruptly and emotionally without further thought. Even if we don't express this emotion externally, we can certainly feel the inner turmoil. When we begin to tame the monkey mind, we will begin to realize that we do not need to react every time we get our buttons pushed. Instead, we can learn to turn down the volume, calm our emotions and take the time to respond as we choose.

Conclusion

For most of us, the monkey mind runs wild and unfettered, often causing mental, emotional and spiritual suffering. Even so, we don't want to get rid of it. It's a necessary part of being human. We need our monkey minds! Instead, we want to understand, train and live in harmony with it.

The first step is to become aware of how the monkey mind works. To be able to see how it is running wild in so many lives, including our own. We want to listen for the voice of our own monkey mind, and begin to interact consciously with it. From there, we can begin to take steps to tame it.

Taming is not hard. It just takes practice.

The practice of taming our monkey mind has many benefits. We will feel so much better. More balanced. Less anxious. Calmer. More intuitive. Happier.

When we take control of our thoughts and become friends with our monkey mind, we become free. Free to be who we really are.

Our life is what our thoughts make it.
Marcus Aurelius

Free yourself from what is holding you back.
Be who you truly are.

THE NEW REALITY

When we are in a state of awareness closer to our true way
of being, this is when we can tangibly feel the New Reality
all around us. And this is when the miracles
and breakthroughs begin!
Solara

I sometimes refer to the *New Reality* in this book. What is the New Reality? Quite simply, it is a shift in focus. This shift is moving from an external focus, which has been the way of life on this planet for a very long time, to an internal focus that is a new way of life.

External Focus

An external focus centers on things, whether that be material possessions, money, fame, fortune, status, career or whatever is wanted from the world. These are the things that humanity has been seeking for fulfillment, for happiness, for what makes us feel good. There is no fundamental internal spiritual connection, only external. As a result, this external focus makes our happiness and fulfillment dependent upon what is happening outside of us, out there somewhere.

Internal Focus

The shift to the New Reality is to a life based on an internal focus. In other words, a fundamental connection with a higher power be it yourself, God, the Universe, angels – whatever or however we want to describe what that energy is. It is not necessary to believe in "God" or anything beyond ourselves to understand this shift. It is about consciously allowing that creative power, whatever that is to us, to work through our life in such a way that happiness and fulfillment and what makes us feel good comes from within.

New Levels of Awareness

The New Reality brings with it new levels of awareness. One level is the understanding that we are all One. The ultimate reality is what is being discussed and debated and gaining acceptance in many aspects with the continued growth of quantum physics and the study of consciousness itself. What is being recognized is that universal consciousness is the formative essence behind all that exists within the Universe. We are all expressions of that universal consciousness. Individual, unique expressions.

It is our free will which allows us to explore our true potential and express our true selves, to transform ourselves from an external focus to an internal focus. This shift in focus is the New Reality.

New Reality Consciousness

New Reality consciousness is something that is growing all over the planet at this time. More and more of us are awakening to the changes and transformations that we wish to make in our lives. We are becoming more aware that we create our own reality.

Our own reality is a reflection of what we believe, think, feel and do. The more strongly we believe, think, feel and do, the more apparent it becomes that our life is a mirror of what we project.

Do we want to be our REAL selves? Are we excited by the idea? Do we want to experience and express our true potential, and find deep inner fulfillment in this life?

It's like the law of physics. The mirror of life will manifest what we want, but not until we decide first, within ourselves, what it is that we truly want. Once we decide, the process can start. Our new lives of authentic self-expression will begin reflecting the New Reality.

Are you in?

There is great value in unlocking the hidden doors within.
There are many treasures to be discovered.

The Five Keys
to Unlocking the REAL You

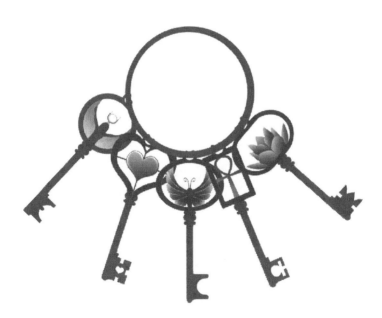

The more the true authentic self can express itself,
the more love and support we invite into our lives.

The Five Keys
to Unlocking the REAL You

Your work is to discover your work and then with
all your heart, give yourself to it.
Buddha

To point us in the direction of our work in becoming more REAL, more authentic, I will be providing some practical ideas and helpful ways to discover and expand on how to do that.

We all wear masks and costumes and assume identities due to our beliefs and conditioning. We think it is who we are, but it's not. It's more about who *they* needed us to be, whoever *they* are or were. Yet all along there is a yearning, a deep longing for something else, for something more ... the REAL you!

The REAL you, your authentic self, wants to come out and play!

The Five Keys to Unlocking the REAL You

The path to becoming the REAL you is not always an easy journey. And it doesn't happen overnight. Anyone who has ever looked inside to see what makes them tick, or even just wondered about it, knows that the work is an ongoing process. It takes courage. It takes persistence. It takes desire.

In order to guide us along the way, and to help make the process much easier, I have identified five keys to unlocking the REAL you.

The five keys are:

1. Accept Yourself

2. Lose the Past

3. Allow Yourself to be Vulnerable

4. Stop Caring What Others Think

5. Be Open and Honest

In the chapters that follow, each key will be explained in detail. If you choose to integrate these keys into your life, they can bring about a level of personal growth and expansion beyond anything you have known before. Using them can help to unlock a greater sense of who you really are, a greater sense of empowerment, a greater sense of purpose, a greater sense of unfolding evolving consciousness, a greater sense of personal freedom, a greater, more expansive and more authentic YOU!

I can say this because I have done this. I have used, and continue to use, these very same practices and processes. I am not saying they are something new. Many of these tools have been around for a long, long time. And for me personally, I have been exploring and learning from them for many decades.

These five keys are the ones that I have personally found to be the most significant and influential to the work I have done to become my true authentic self. To be the REAL Darity. And I'm happy to now be able to share them. To help guide and support you in becoming the REAL you!

It Comes From the Heart

Your heart is the size of an ocean.
Go find yourself in its hidden depths.
Rumi

Becoming the REAL you comes from the heart. It is an outflow of becoming authentic. This does not mean in any way, shape or form that you are just like everyone or anyone else. It is really just you becoming a broader and more expansive version of yourself. It brings peace and congruence.

This journey provides challenges and opportunities for us to gain deeper meaning from our emotions, to draw boundaries with people who are toxic, to better nurture and care for ourselves. It is probably the most challenging and the most rewarding journey possible. I hope you will enjoy the adventure. Thank you for joining me.

Let's begin!

It is only when we learn about ourselves, and begin to really know ourselves, that we can begin to accept ourselves.

Key #1

ACCEPT YOURSELF

*The curious paradox is that when I accept myself
just as I am, then I can change.*
Carl Rogers

One of the keys that unlocks the door of self-discovery, along the path of becoming more of who we really are, is that of accepting ourselves. Yep, it seems everyone understands the importance of this practice, yet putting the key in the lock, actually turning it, and moving on through is pretty much avoided at all costs. We may find, once we start, that it is a lifelong experience. It took me many, many years to move into complete self-acceptance, and it is something I still have to constantly monitor.

Warts and All

The first step on the road of accepting ourselves, to become the REAL you, is to start by just doing it. Being able to say, *I accept myself right here, right now, warts and all.* This is where we start.

It sounds straightforward, yet I can easily share that accepting myself has been one of the most difficult things I have ever done. Though not easy, it is definitely a key. It is a necessary step to grow and evolve and become. Starting to look at myself, warts and all, is where I began. This is where we all begin.

I grew up with a significant lack of self-esteem due to my self-imposed conditioned belief that I was totally unlovable. That is how I felt most of the early part of my life. Having experienced abandonment at an early age, I concluded I was just not worthy of anything. Even when my mother came and got me from the foster homes, I felt totally unsure of myself in this new world. I had a new step-father. We moved a lot and I got a new sister. It felt like constant chaos for a little girl.

Real or not, I felt and incorporated the belief that I was no good because no one had wanted me. And I believed that I couldn't trust anyone at all, for anything. In order for me to shift my beliefs to a place of self-acceptance, I had to begin by looking at myself right where I was at the time, warts and all.

We certainly all have different stories about why we feel we are not good enough or smart enough or good-looking enough. Either self-imposed or conditioned by parents or others. There are also those beliefs that we unconsciously made up based on what happened when we were young. We tend to hold those beliefs for a very long time. Each of these types of beliefs interfere with our ability to accept ourselves.

When we start on the path of self-discovery, we give ourselves the opportunity to look and see if the beliefs we have about ourselves still apply. If yes, we keep them. If no, we can change them. Once we start on that path, there is no turning back.

I Love You, I Love You, I Love You

I remember when I was early on this path of self-acceptance, I read in one of my spiritual books how important it is to love yourself. That was a stunner for me. I barely liked myself, how the heck was I ever going to love myself? I can tell you today as I sit here and write these words that it is so. I love who I am. I love where I am. And I love, love, love what I am doing!

If you don't currently love, love, love everything about your life, hang in there. Keep at getting to the REAL you and watch your life blossom more and more every day. You can do it!

Practice: Self-Acceptance Mirror

A practice that really moved me along the path of self-acceptance sounded goofy to me when I first read about it. The process is looking in the mirror and saying, *I love you.* Goofy or not, I was determined to begin and decided, what the hay, let's see if it works.

Looking at myself in the mirror, I would practice this saying over and over again: *I love you, I love you, I love you.* I'll never forget the first time I did it. I looked deep into my own eyes with such immense love for who I am. I was surprised because I could see my pupils dilating as I said the words *I love you, I love you, I love you* ... I could feel the love flowing through me. There, behind the façade, behind the human mask, behind the mind, there I was! This immense love resonated throughout my body all the way to my tailbone, to my root chakra, to my soul.

Needless to say, I found this to be a wonderful practice of self-acceptance, and highly recommend it.

Try it out. Right now. Don't worry about feeling goofy. (I sure did the first time!) Go to a mirror, right this moment. Say the words, *I love you*, over and over again. Watch what happens!

Has anyone ever looked into your eyes, into your soul, like you just did, and told you that they loved you? If someone has, you are immensely fortunate. The fact that you just told yourself makes you extremely blessed. Love always starts from within.

Assess Our Values

What we value makes up
the essence of who we are.

Another key to accepting ourselves is to assess our values. To figure out what is really most important to us. To determine what has the greatest value, here and now, today. Not yesterday or tomorrow, but right at this very moment.

This process, this practice of taking the time to think about and feel what has the most value to us, is an important part of learning how to accept ourselves.

In order to assess our values, we may have to think about it. We may have to ask ourselves some basic questions. For example: *How do I view the world? Is it a good place? Bad place? Both? Am I a good person? What parts of my life are important to me? Friends? Family? School? Career? Church? Money? Fame? Which one is the most important? Do I have any addictions? Drugs? Sex? Gambling? Alcohol? Food? Other? What do I value most in my life? What is most important to me?*

We need to take an honest look at everything in our life. This is for us alone. It is not something we necessarily share with others. We want to be able to explore ourselves freely and honestly.

It is only when we learn about ourselves, and begin to really know ourselves, that we can begin to accept ourselves.

Evaluating Values: A Personal Story

The following is a personal story from my own journey. It is one that helped me to review and evaluate my values. It was a process I didn't even realize I needed to do until I was in the midst of it.

Many years ago I ran for the United States Congress. During this time, as I travelled around speaking to many different groups of people, I discovered that I wanted to be everything to everybody. I had lived the early part of my life this way, so it was an easy trap for me to fall into. But, hey, I wanted everyone to vote for me, right? It got really crazy confusing for me after a bit of that. I got really scattered. I recognized that I could not be everything to everybody. I felt this was really impacting my integrity.

Now, keep in mind that integrity in politics was something that has always been important to me. In fact, it was one of the main reasons I even ran for Congress. I wanted to bring much needed integrity to the table.

Feeling my integrity was at risk, as I tried to be all things to all people, I found myself not being authentically me. That did not feel good at all. So, I took some quiet meditative time to deeply reflect upon what I truly believed politically, philosophically, personally. I don't think I had ever done that before. It was a very interesting experience. It gave me a boost of confidence and a much greater understanding. Not only about myself as a person, but also about what I stood for. I knew that what I stood for was what caused me to stop my life and throw my hat into the political arena in the first place. So, game on!

From that experience, I created an *I Believe* speech. It gave me the ability to share the real, true me with others, while also retaining my integrity. It was a hit and became my stump speech. Not only did it let me share myself with potential voters, it also helped me to be true to myself. And that felt good! I truly learned more about who I AM. I was then able to say confidently and unapologetically, to those who did not agree with my positions on issues: Then I would not be the person you would vote for.

Personality Tests

The process of learning more about ourselves is an ongoing and valuable practice. In addition to being introspective, there are many ways to obtain information about ourselves from places that are outside of ourselves. One way is through personality tests.

We can gain a lot of insight about who we are by exploring the many personality tests that are available. They can also be fun and provide a benchmark for us. Some folks take them regularly and save them over the years, so they can see the progress of their changes.

One thing about personality tests to be aware of is that they are subjective. It is also important to make sure that we do not let them define us. We are dynamic beings, changing all the time, never static, always growing and evolving.

Personality tests are tools that can give us a more in-depth vision of ourselves, or reveal something about ourselves that we may not have noticed. At the very least, they can provide inspiration for further self-discovery.

Becoming Conscious of Our Consciousness

Another method of discovering the REAL you is to become more conscious of ourselves behind the mind. What does that mean? It means we check out what we are *feeling* as opposed to what we are *thinking*.

We all tend to be so locked up in the mind. As we continue to learn about ourselves, and seek to better understand who we really are, we are challenged to move beyond that. To realize that we are not the mind. We are not our thoughts. We are not our body, a bag of skin. We are the consciousness behind and within all of that.

Becoming more conscious of ourselves makes it possible to reach new levels of understanding. We are able to truly experience that we are neither our mind nor our body. This is a big step on the path of self-discovery. Of stepping more fully into our true authentic selves.

As we begin to move beyond the belief that what we think about, that internal dialogue going on inside our head, is us, we can realize that we are the presence *behind* the mind. That is our real true self. The real true self is the one listening to the mind do its thing.

What??? We are not the mind? We are not the body? We are the consciousness of the mind and of the body??? Okay, if that sounds crazy, if this concept is new, then I suggest spending some time with the idea. At least contemplate it. It is truly a different feeling. A big shift in perception. Why is that? Because most of us weren't conditioned to have that belief. We weren't brought up with the awareness or the understanding of it. It's a different perspective than we knew before.

Becoming Conscious of Our Feelings

As conscious beings, we are always feeling something. Due to my upbringing, I shut down my feelings most of my life. I remember at one point thinking, *Do I feel anything at all?* I had repressed so much to protect myself. Feeling was painful. It took a lot of work for me to find my feelings, and from there to bring them into my consciousness to be examined. Once I was able to really see them, and begin to understand them, then I made the conscious choice to either release and surrender them, or, in some cases, to integrate and open them more.

In order for us to become more conscious of our feelings, and to move in the direction of self-acceptance, we need to be able to explore our feelings up close and personal.

Ask yourself: *How are you with your feelings? Open? Closed? Numb? Do you embrace what you feel? Or avoid it?*

There is no right or wrong answer here, only the deepening of the relationship to self. Many of us avoid our feelings because it is just too painful.

The practice of becoming more conscious of our feelings requires us to look at them, one by one, and to see if what we are feeling is real or if it is a conditioned response. To really notice what we are feeling. Maybe what we are feeling is actually something our parents, friends, co-workers taught us to feel. Or maybe it's how we thought we were supposed to feel, or were taught to feel. So the question becomes: What do we *really* feel?

Awareness Exercise: Exploring Our Feelings

In order to experience this now, take a moment to notice what thoughts and feelings come up:

What kind of judgments do you make based on feelings about race? What about gender? Sexual orientation? Nationality? Tall people? Short people? Fat people? Thin people? Pretty people? Ugly people? Smart people? Not so smart people?

Are you making these judgments because someone told you this is the way it is and you believed them?

Has your family upbringing or religion told you thus and so about it but you have never actually questioned how you really feel about it? How do you really feel?

Exploring our feelings is about tapping into how our real true self feels, not what someone told us to feel or not to feel or what to believe or not to believe.

The next practice of being conscious of ourselves on the journey of self-acceptance is taking a look at how we treat ourselves with the power of language.

The Power of Language

The power of language, our thoughts and our words, is so much more important than we previously knew. It literally creates our reality. Therefore it is important how we talk to ourselves and to others.

If we understood the power of our thoughts,
we would guard them more closely. If we understood the
awesome power of our words, we would prefer silence to almost
anything negative. In our thoughts and words we create our own
weaknesses and our own strengths. Our limitations and joys begin
in our hearts. We can always replace negative with positive.
Betty J. Eadie

Become Conscious of Our Internal Dialog

In today's information filled world, most everyone is aware of the concept of internal dialogue or just the fact that we talk to ourselves. We can laugh, and I often do, about my inside voice and my outside voice. *I did not just say that, did I? Must have been my inside voice.* It is always good for a laugh and yet, this inside voice is just how we analyze our feelings about ourselves and what it is we wish to change to feel better about who we are, and learn to love ourselves.

From my own journey of self-acceptance, I remember the first time I heard the words *internal dialogue.* I was blown away. *What? I said to myself. Really? That is what that is? Wow!* I had just never had the realization that it was me talking to myself inside my head, let alone me listening to myself. I was relatively young when this concept came to me. I am glad for it. It helped so much in the first steps to becoming myself.

So, how does this play out?

The analysis begins by listening to ourselves. It might be a good thing to write down what you discover as you explore the internal dialogue. Become aware of the patterns and what I call *ruts of thought* about who we are and what we are about. If we are not conscious of our thoughts on ourselves, we can be pretty mean to ourselves and not even be aware of it. I know I was, for sure! It can be a shocking revelation to hear not only what we have to say to ourselves, yet also the tone we say it in.

The way we talk to our children
becomes their inner voice.
Peggy O'Mara

This exploration revolves around looking at how we phrase things to ourselves. Does it sound like Mom, Dad, Brother, Sister, Teacher, Pastor, Priest, Friend? Something someone told us? Something we have heard before? Something we just accepted as true? If so, be sure to check that out. That is the only way to begin to change it up.

By becoming aware of our internal dialogue, we then have the opportunity to change it. Are the words we hear inside our heads positive or negative? Are we hearing such things as: *You are wonderful. You are amazing. You can do anything you want. You will have great success in your life?* Or are we hearing: *You are stupid. You are worthless. You can't do anything right. You will never amount to anything?* Take time to notice.

Whether they are positive or negative, most of the statements we hear inside our head are generally something we were told and we accepted when we were growing up.

Paying attention to our inner dialogue allows us to become more aware of how we treat ourselves, which we may not even be conscious of at the moment.

Become Conscious of How We Treat Ourselves

To look at how we treat ourselves, we begin with how we talk to ourselves about ourselves. This is an interesting and important analysis.

How do we do that?

We begin by consciously listening to ourselves. Listening to our internal dialogue.

This internal dialogue, in particular what we say to ourselves about ourselves, can provide us with lots of opportunities to change how we feel inside. We will talk about other kinds of internal dialogue when we discuss the fifth key of being open and honest.

Most of us have been taught that it is inappropriate to brag, so we avoid saying anything positive, even to ourselves. Yet it is an important analysis. Is what we are saying to ourselves positive or is it negative? Are we complaining about ourselves? What kinds of words do we use regularly? Are we loving, mean, kind, unkind, angry, sympathetic? Are they the words of others that we have chosen to accept as our own? This is the analysis for self-talk.

Over the course of my personal journey, I have worked many years on not being so hard on myself. I listened to my internal dialogue. I found the practice of stopping that internal dialogue when it started demeaning me, for whatever reason. This has resulted in a regular practice of self-compassion, a nice balance of heart and mind. An inner peace. I stepped into a place of acceptance of the here and now. This gave me the ability to be nicer to myself, no matter what was going on.

Being nicer to ourselves harmonizes our inner space and brings us a peaceful co-existence with our monkey mind and our heart. It's about working together. It does take time. There are no easy pills for this. The practice of monitoring our thoughts, exercising self-compassion and observing the way we treat ourselves can change everything.

Evaluate Our Internal Dialogue

Once we become more aware of our internal dialogue, whether it is positive or negative, the next step is to evaluate our internal arena. Keeping in mind the goal of self-acceptance.

If it makes us feel good and more accepting of ourselves, we keep it. If it makes us feel bad or not good about ourselves, then it is something we might want to jettison. How do we do that? It becomes another practice, of course.

Practice: Stop It in Its Tracks

We have talked about this practice before, in the chapter about the monkey mind. It's about the practice of yelling *Stop!* In that chapter we reviewed different methods that can be used to distract the monkey mind. My intent in this chapter is to formalize the practice a little more, showing how the repeated use of this practice not only distracts, but can also be used to create a new thought pattern.

The process is, every time the negative pattern of thought arises that makes us feel bad, we stop it in its tracks. It's usually our monkey mind at work. We know we are in charge of what goes on with the internal dialogue. We may just not have realized it yet. Or we may just not have exercised it yet!

So how do we stop it in its tracks? We just say, *Stop!*

Of course we have to mean it. Seriously mean it.

I wish I could say that's all it takes, just one bold *Stop!* However, as with most spiritual practices, it's a process. We will probably have to do it over and over, every time the negative thought pattern arises. And that will probably be many, many times. However, with consistent use of this practice, the negative thought pattern will truly begin to show up less and less and less, and eventually fade away.

What I love about this practice is that it not only stops the negative thinking in its tracks, but it also provides us with the opportunity to replace it with new thoughts, ones that we want to have instead. Thoughts that make us feel good.

It becomes a feeling thing. We want to feel good, and part of feeling good is thinking good thoughts about ourselves. This, then, reflects in our lives by us becoming the cause of our own feelings rather than the effect of them. At the same time it opens our hearts more and more.

Become Conscious of How We Talk About Ourselves

I hear folks all the time demeaning, criticizing and complaining about themselves in front of others: *I'm so stupid. I'm such a klutz. I can't do anything right. I'm such a loser. I always mess things up. What a dummy.* How can we ever accept ourselves when we not only think such negative thoughts, but then also confirm those thoughts by saying them out loud?

It is important to observe how we talk out loud about ourselves in the company of others. To become more aware. If we catch ourselves saying something negative about ourselves in front of others, we can use the same *Stop It in Its Tracks* method. Simply stop speaking, even mid-sentence. Or immediately pause and turn it around on the spot, saying something positive instead.

Always remember that words have power. That is the reason why the way we talk about ourselves matters. As we move along the path of self-acceptance, we can make a conscious choice to be kinder to ourselves with our words.

Words to Watch Out For

Working with the use of words becomes especially important as we move along the path of self-discovery. Part of our work in accepting ourselves is to clean up our language. As we become more and more conscious of our inner dialogue, we can begin to examine the specific word choices that we are using.

Let's begin by taking a closer look at some common words that we might want to consider eliminating.

The Word: But

Sansa Stark:
They respect you, they really do, but you have to ...
Why are you laughing?

Jon Snow:
What did father use to say?
Everything before the word "but" is horse shit.
Game of Thrones, Season 7, Episode 1

Let's look more closely at the word **but**.

Generally speaking, the word *but* negates the prior statement. It is also like the word *try*, which we will also talk about, in the sense that it can similarly give you an opportunity to not accomplish something. It can make an excuse. It can change intentions and even actions.

Mostly we do not even realize the power of the word *but*. There are lots of articles about boycotting the word *but*, and I am in full agreement. I definitely work at it. Changing it up when I can.

Since I am particularly attuned to it, I catch folks using it all the time to negate the prior statement. Here's an example used by a politician: *His policy is important, but ...* In this example, by use of the word *but*, the speaker has implied that the most important thing is really whatever follows the word *but*. The use of the word *but* negates the importance of the policy.

Some other examples we can be attuned to include:

I love you, but ...

You are a great friend, but ...

I value your honesty, but ...

In these examples, by using the word *but*, the speaker has implied that whatever follows the word *but* is more important than love, or friendship, or honesty. The word *but* negates the importance of the words that precede it.

The word *but* can also be used as an excuse. Some examples include:

I want to get in shape, but ...

I should go on a date, but ...

I could try to do it, but ...

Sometimes we can be oblivious to the fact that by using the word *but* we are negating the prior statement and are simply providing an excuse.

This works great if we want to verbalize our weaknesses, but it does nothing to promote our confidence and sense of well-being. (See, I did that one on purpose!)

The Words: Always and Never

Always and never are two words you should always remember never to use.
Wendell Johnson

Now let's look at the words **always** and **never**. *Always* and *never* statements are most often used by people arguing to illustrate the merits of their position. They are generalizations.

Here are a few examples we can be attuned to:

You always have to have the last word.

You never listen to me.

You are always shouting at me.

You never really try.

I always give you what you want.

Always and *never* statements are exaggerations and not literal. They don't allow for any exceptions; they don't leave any room for *sometimes* or *occasionally* or *mostly*.

In my personal life, when someone tells me I always or never do such and so, I *always* remind them that it is not true, ever. I *never* do anything *always!*

Another important consideration is that *always* and *never* tend to send strong signals which may have a negative impact on the person to whom they are being said. These words can hurt other people's feelings, which is either an unconscious or conscious intent. Perhaps we want to think about changing that up.

Some *always* and *never* statements are used in an accusatory or self-pitying way, usually in an attempt to invoke a sympathetic response:

You never wanted me.

You always hated me.

You never really loved me.

There is a self-contradicting adage that says: *Always and never statements are always false and never true.*

It is a helpful practice to observe how or if we use these words, both as part of our inner dialogue and also as part of how we speak to others. Once we become aware, we can then make the choice to reduce or eliminate the use of *always* and *never* from our vocabulary.

The Word: Try

Try not. Do, or do not. There is no try.
Yoda

Now let's look at the word **try**. The word *try* implies failure and, here again, provides an excuse.

I will try to meet up with you.

I will try to do it.

I will try to open the shop early.

I will try to be on time.

And finally, there is absolutely no commitment to the word try.

Well, I tried …

See. There is no commitment. It is merely an attempt to provide a disclaimer up front in case of failure. This weakens the power of our words.

I call *try* a weasel word and try to catch myself every time I begin to say it. What? Did I just use it? See how sneaky *try* is? What I meant to say is I <u>work on</u> catching myself every time.

I remember the first time I became aware of the issue with the word *try*. It was when I attended a Transactional Analysis seminar, many years ago. The way they demonstrated the concept was by using the word *try* in the following sentence:

I'll try to get you a glass of water.

Huh? See, it makes no sense. You are either going to get me a glass of water, or you are not. You either do something or you do not, just as Yoda says. There is no try.

The Word: Should

Don't should yourself.
Wendy Kaveney

The word **should** is another good word to consider removing from our vocabulary, or at least a word to start paying attention to, both internally and externally. I have had a lot of practice with this one!

The word *should* may occasionally give good guidance, but mostly it sets up unrealistic expectations. It can cause guilt and anxiety and decrease our desire to do what we might otherwise really want to do.

Sure, we *should* take good care of ourselves and our kids. We *should* pay our bills. We *should* be honest. Yet most of the time when we use the word *should* it is disempowering and can actually undermine what we really want to do. We can end up causing ourselves undue pain, guilt and anxiety with *should*.

Here are some examples:

I should have gone to the meeting ...

You should have turned in your application on time ...

We should have delivered it in person ...

The word *should* also conveys a sense or a feeling that someone or something outside of ourselves is trying to control us, to tell us what to do, to try and make us feel bad if we don't do it. Which, if you are like me, can trigger a rebellious nature. *If I have to do it, I won't. If I should do it, then maybe I will, maybe I won't. No one is going to tell me what I should or should not do!* This can create an ambivalent feeling of stress for some of us.

As we become more and more aware of the language we use, we can add the practice of noticing when we *should* ourselves to the list, and ~~try to~~ eliminate it from our vocabulary.

And finally, on the brighter side, there are some words that we actually want to add to our vocabulary! Let's take a look ...

The Words: I Am, I Can, I Have

As we become more consciously aware of our internal and external dialogue, we discover that we can replace negative words with positive words. We can choose to use words that are uplifting and affirming, words like **I am, I can, I have.** These are some of the most powerful words we can use because they direct our thoughts. Depending on what follows those words, they can have a significant impact on who we are and who we are becoming. Therefore, the words that follow *I am, I can, I have* become very potent words, essentially creating our reality.

Here are some examples:

I am confident that ...

I can achieve ...

I have the ability to ...

Awareness Leads to Change

Checking out our internal dialogue is one way of becoming more conscious of ourselves and, therefore, more able to accept ourselves. Pay attention. Listen to what we say to ourselves in the privacy of our own minds. And also listen to what we say out loud in the company of others.

When we become more conscious and aware of the words we use, and recognize the affect they have upon us and others, we can then choose to consciously change it up. We can choose words that make us feel better about ourselves, words that promote self-acceptance.

Accepting Ourselves

Being able to love and accept ourselves is part of the spiritual foundation for being a more authentic, REAL you. The path of self-acceptance takes time. It is a process. It challenges us to embrace ourselves, warts and all. To explore our deep inner feelings and our values. It asks us to become more aware of our own internal and external dialogue, and to become more conscious of the words we chose. Once we become aware, then we have the power to change whatever it is that we wish to change. The choice is ours. These choices are the ones that will lead us to greater self-acceptance, which is one of the essential keys to becoming the REAL you!

Key #2

LOSE THE PAST

You can only lose what you cling to.
Buddha

This key to unlocking the REAL you is all about learning how to focus on the present moment, and not on the past. This includes thoughts and feelings about how we used to be, who we used to love, what happened to us, what we may have done to others, what others may have done to us. All the good, the bad and the ugly.

We do, of course, continue to carry the memories of who we used to be, how we used to act, what happened to us and what we did. It's good to applaud our growth from those stages, especially when we see the changes we have made along the way. We really are the only ones who can determine that. In that determination, we no longer need to identify with any of our past. It does not need to influence how we should, or could, or would act now.

Turn Our Focus to the Present Moment

This idea is that when we lose the past, we are able to turn our focus more fully to the present moment. So much of our lives are completely preoccupied with either the past, including memories, or the future, including expectations or fantasies of what will be.

When we shift our focus to being present in the here and now, we can feel deep in our souls that there never was, nor will there ever be, any other experience than the present moment. What we truly feel in this moment is what is real. Not what we think we are supposed to feel or what we have been taught or conditioned to feel.

Times have definitely changed. We have definitely changed. And things are now changing every day. Letting go of what and how it used to be is a big step in the self-discovery adventure.

Are We Living in the Past?

I find a lot of people are living in the past. Maybe even without realizing it. Wishing for the ways things were instead of how they are now. Why would we want to change that? Because the past is gone. Whatever we are wishing for is no more. There is no going back. Be it yesterday, last month, last year or way back to when we were children. No matter how we frame it, it is no more.

The past is simply a mental construct. Something that is only in the mind. It does evoke feelings, emotions, thoughts and memories. These feelings, emotions, thoughts and memories bring back the sensations of times gone by. However, they are not real. They do not exist. And dwelling on them is not conducive to our personal and spiritual growth.

I am not saying we have to forget everything we've experienced or that we have to pretend the past did not happen. We all have many memories of times gone by. Good memories. Bad memories. Special moments. What's important to realize is that spending a lot of time reliving those experiences creates patterns in the mind. These patterns are particularly helpful for the monkey mind to continually travel, evoking feelings of nostalgia or sadness or pain or a wide variety of other familiar emotions.

We don't want to continue to create who we have been in the past. We want to drop all that and step more fully into who we are now, and who we are becoming.

Ruts That Keep Us Stuck

Our monkey mind uses these stored memories of the past to distract us. To get us off track and out of the present moment. Dwelling on those thoughts and feelings of the past, swinging from branch to branch of past experiences, causes those ruts in our thinking that need to be broken out of. Those persistent ruts, those patterns of thought, take us down the same roads of the hurts, the pain, the sadness, the nostalgia, and to no avail.

Sometimes, of course, those ruts go the other way, wishing for those *good old days* (high school, college, boyfriend, girlfriend, whatever) again. *Oh, they were so good and life is so awful now! I want to go back to those carefree days.* No matter which patterns or ruts of thoughts of the past we go down, and we usually have a sufficient supply of both, they are not of value for us on our quest for authenticity and trueness. Why? Because they hold us back. They distract us from creating whatever it is we want. They keep us stuck. Not moving forward. We want to move forward to be the best we can be. Yes? Yes.

Life is like monkey bars.
You have to let go to move forward.
Anonymous

Are We on the Bow or Stern of Our Life Boat?

Many years ago, while on my personal quest for authenticity and trueness, I read many of Wayne Dyer's early works. I remember him addressing the concept of losing the past. It made a big impression on me and I integrated it into my life at that point. He used the analogy that our life is a boat. If we are standing in the back of the boat looking back, off the stern, then we cannot see where we are going, nor can we direct the boat to where we want to go. Good, eh?

The point being, of course, is that as we look back, as we dwell on the past and on who we were, what happened to us, what we did, instead of being in the boat paying attention to where we are going, we really stop growing. If we are focused on the past, we don't know where we are going or what we are doing. We are unable to live the full life we all really want.

Defining Ourselves in Time

Another aspect of this particular key of losing the past, is to explore ourselves honestly. Do we define ourselves by a certain period in our life? So many people do. For instance, you may have heard people say, or may even say it yourself: *Ah, in high school I was so popular. I was a cheerleader* (played football, was in band, whatever) *and involved in so many social activities. Everyone loved me. Those were the best days of my life.* Or, *Oh my college days were the best time in my life. I had so many friends. I went places; I did things. I had so much fun. Life was so much better then.* Or, *When I was little, my Mommy loved me so very much; she took such good care of me. We had such wonderful vacations. My brothers or sisters were with me and we were all so close. Those were the best times of my life!*

The question for us to ask ourselves is, *Do we define ourselves by a certain period in our life?* Think about it. *Are we still wearing the same hair style, the same kind of clothes, using the same language? Do we long to go back to those wonderful times?*

Living in the Past Can Make Us Stagnant

The truth is, those wonderful times may not really have been so wonderful at the time, at least not as wonderful as our memory seems to recall. But no matter what, if we let those mental constructs, those things that no longer exist, define who we are now, then we are not being our true selves. We are not living in the present moment. If we let the past define us, then we are not able to recognize what changes have taken place. We are not able to see who we are now, or what our life is showing us we can be. When this happens, we become stagnant.

We are dynamic evolving human beings. Becoming stagnant is not good for our mental, physical or spiritual health. We each have the opportunity to evolve on a micro-cosmic and macro-cosmic scale like never before. Yep, I know, that means changing.

Yikes!

Resisting Change

Now, I admit it is true. A lot of people, maybe even most of us, resist change. We can probably all agree that change is one of the hardest things to do. Especially personal change. It is not easy to look inside ourselves and begin to change things. I know. It is certainly easier, or at least more comfortable, to just go along being buffeted by the experiences of life as they come. Being reactive rather that responsive. It is way easier to not confront ourselves, to not make ourselves do the work to make us more authentic. But a lot of times we don't do it simply because we just don't know any better.

From the moment you become aware that
you have a choice, you do.
Ingrid Coffin

There really is a choice in everything. Yet, no one told us. No one told us we don't have to stay the same. No one told us we don't have to remain a victim. No one told us we don't have to be buffeted around by life. No one told us we had a choice. Usually we were told just the opposite, *That's just the way it is.*

"It's Just the Way I Am"

So often when I have shared with others the truth that we can change anything we want to about ourselves, people have said to me: *Oh, that's just the way I am.* Or *Oh, that's just my nature.* Really? You think so? You're just stuck with it? Nothing more to be said then. That's all there is to it. End of conversation. Right? Nah, I don't think so!

The real truth is we CAN change. We do it all the time. We can feel good. We can have confidence. We can know that we are grounded and evolving. The truth of the matter is, it does not have to be the end of the conversation. There is absolutely no need to be *just the way you are.* I suppose it is certainly easier and more comfortable than to make choices and changes. Yet that generally means staying the same, feeling the same, not growing and evolving. *Does that give us confidence? Does that give us freedom? Does that give us the opportunity to be all we want to be, and more?* You decide.

If, as Socrates said, *The unexamined life is not worth living,* we have the opportunity to explore who we really are at any time.

The truth is, we are not one certain way all the time. We feel and behave in different ways depending on where we are, who we are with, what we are doing, the mood we are in, and so forth. We have different sides of ourselves. Whether it be day or night, summer or fall, alone or with friends, with this friend or that friend, in meetings, at work, at the bar, at the game, with the kids, with our significant other, by ourselves. In each case we feel and behave differently. Yet, it is all us.

We alone decide who we are and who we want to be in each and every present moment. The key is to lose the past. To give up our ideas about who we were then and be who we are now. Who we are now may be different from who we were then, or maybe not. It depends on the situation or the relationship or how long ago it was. But exploring ourselves honestly and making those choices are keys to this step.

"I Am Nothing Without You"
Really???

Another key to losing the past is to see if we define ourselves by our past relationships. I have heard so often from people that a person from their past *completes them* or *makes them whole* or was their *soul-mate.* That they miss having so-and-so in their life. That so-and-so broke up with them or divorced them and without that person they can't go on. Nothing ever gets better because so-and-so is not here, left me, whatever.

So how does this play out? Check out if this, or something like it, is what our monkey mind is telling us: *Oh, when I was with him/her life was so good. I was a loving, caring, and compassionate person. The world was my oyster. I could do anything. Or, I need this person so much, I cannot go on without them in my life, they complete me! I want them back!*

Does this sound like the monkey mind at work?

Losing the Past of a Past Relationship

Fantasizing about how wonderful life was then, or about how we cannot possibly live without someone from the past, is the type of thought pattern that keeps us from moving forward.

So how do we get past them?

First, recognize that this is a thought pattern, a mental construct. It is a thought form. The relationship no longer exists the same as it did then. We have convinced ourselves that this is the way it is. Yet, it is only in the recognition of it as a thought form, and nothing more, that we can begin to make the changes necessary to move on from that perspective.

It is past. Lose it! How?

Every time the thought of this person begins to creep into our thoughts, stop it and say, *No! It's over! I'm not going there!* And don't. This is part of managing and taming the monkey mind.

The Loss of a Loved One

Sometimes we find that the perspective of defining ourselves by a relationship, or even by a period of time in our life, may relate to a loved one who has died. And that grief continues to hold us to the past.

I am not at all insensitive to the pain of the grief of losing loved ones, even furry ones. In my own life, I have certainly had that experience, myself, many times. From the loss of a baby to the loss of my parents, siblings, close friends, furry friends and others. I would never, ever, presume to say that we have to forget about those whom we have loved, those who have left the planet, as part of losing the past.

What I would say, however, is that it is important that we not dwell on or make up fantasies in the mind about what could have, would have, should have been with a loved one who has died. When we dwell on those kinds of thoughts it generates emotions which hurt us. It keeps us stuck. It continues the grief and slows down the healing potential.

Losing the Past Does Not Mean Forgetting

The healing comes when we allow the pain, the grief, the sadness to be felt. We have to honor our emotions and let them release. It is what helps us heal. We do not need the monkey mind making up scenarios for our dead loved ones to play a part in. They are gone from this physical world. We miss them terribly! Yet, to hang on to playing scenes with them, *Oh if they were only here to see this or that,* dismisses the fact that they may or may not, in fact, be here and seeing that. Maybe they are seeing it from a different perspective, eh?

It is my belief, from a spiritual, metaphysical experience, that they really are always with us. They are just in non-physical form. If we allow this belief to be part of our experience, we are able to slowly but surely, over time, lose the pain and the grief. We never, ever, lose the love or the memories. Losing the past does not mean forgetting about our loved ones.

Practice: Honoring Those Who Have Passed

While we are on this subject, I would like to share something that I do to honor those who have passed. It's quite special to me.

I have put the dates of the passing of all my loved ones, friends and family and furry ones, on the calendar, along with the year they passed. Every year it comes up on my calendar and I spend the day with them. Loving them, thinking of them, sending them my best wishes and remembering that they were a part of my life. I look forward to being with them again when I'm done here.

This is a practice that I really love and I am happy to share it with you. I have found as I have done this over the years, that it allows me to move forward and yet not forget. I spend that day in honor of their lives, and how they have touched mine.

The Healing Comes

I have seen so many people who have been unable to get past their grief. It carries on year after year after year. I certainly know how that is. When we allow just the grief to influence our feelings, and not allow our monkey mind to manipulate them, then the grief – the real pain of the loss – gets less and less. And we heal.

In my own experience of grief, I lost a baby that I had carried and loved and related to in-utero for nine months and two weeks. He was dead when I went into labor. Oh my goodness, the pain, the anguish, the loss, the grief.

After a long period of grief, I found that every year on April 21st I would remember and cry and cry for the loss. That went on for about 21 years and then one year it passed right on by. I noticed it a couple of weeks later and said, *Wow, I missed it. The grief, the pain is gone.* I learned it can happen. The pain can go away. Not the memories, but the pain. So while it is an old adage that time heals all wounds, I found this to be true about the wounds of the past in relationship to grief.

Now, I am quite aware that the experience I had with my stillborn baby was not a teenage son, or my beloved husband, or the closest person in my heart, as I never knew my son. Yet I have found the same to be true with the death of my mother, who was so close in my heart that I had a quickening behind my heart at the moment of her death. I had many, many, many years of weeping whenever I thought of her.

Over the years, I have found that what I called my *Mom attacks*, the indiscriminate sadness and weeping, seemed to slow down and, eventually, were pretty much over. Certainly not the love or the memories, but the grief, the pain, is gone.

Letting Go

Some of us think holding on makes us strong,
but sometimes it is letting go.
Hermann Karl Hesse

What?! Letting go makes us strong? Why is that? I think it has to do with not holding on to the past. Allowing feelings to come when they do and then letting them go, allowing them to move on. Not manipulating them in the mind, not keeping the pain alive by going back to the old days, the memories. But massaging it by allowing the pain out at every chance you get.

What is the practice? It is about letting it all go. There are times to let go, especially of the past. Allow yourself the space to change and grow. To improve and develop. To become wiser.

Getting Help

If we find it is too difficult or just too painful to work through these emotions ourselves, we may need some extra help. There are lots of mental health professionals who can help us through letting go of relationships that we think define us, or releasing the grief from the loss of loved ones. There are also books available and support groups that we can join, in person or on-line. By taking whatever steps are needed for our own healing process, we are affirming a desire to feel better and to move forward. This is what activates the healing process.

Grieving in Our Own Way

When we are working our way through the grieving process, it is important to recognize that at no time are we trying to forget about our loved one. Taking steps to ease our own pain and grief does not disrespect them or besmirch their memory in any way.

Even if others expect us to act a certain way, know that it is our own heart, our own spirit, our own emotions that we must live with and deal with. Other people's expectations of how we should grieve have nothing to do with us. We want to be our REAL selves and this means we allow ourselves to grieve in our own way, at our own pace. This allows the healing process to work best for us.

Taking Better Care of Ourselves

The work here is to step to the next level of understanding that our most important relationship is with ourselves. Yep. It is true everything really IS about us!

Generally speaking, we have been told for years that we are not important. We have been told that it is selfish to think only of ourselves or to think of ourselves first. More and more folks are now awakening to the reality that we cannot really be of service to anyone else unless we are able to take care of ourselves first.

That is what we are doing here with this book. We are learning how to take better care of ourselves. We are learning to be kinder to ourselves, and to value ourselves more. This is essential to becoming our REAL selves. This will bring more joy, peace, understanding and compassion into our lives.

A big part of becoming who we really are is about strengthening the relationship we have with ourselves. This generally includes cutting emotional ties to those who are no longer part of our lives, whether by choice or happenstance. This is a very important concept to understand. We talked about it when we explored the key of accepting ourselves. And it is also a big part of the key of losing the past.

I want to share a book I read a long time ago. It is called _The Art of Selfishness_ by David Seabury. This book discusses how to work on honoring our relationship to self. At a personal development level, as well as a spiritual level, it is only when we have become whole within ourselves that we are able to have wholeness with another. And even then it takes a lot of work to keep it real.

The Power of Forgiveness

The last practice in letting go of the past is to incorporate and exercise forgiveness. I'm sure we have all heard that before, how important it is to forgive. And yes, it's really true!

Forgiveness is an important basis for spiritual work. It asserts and recognizes that we can truly know and appreciate only our own life's journey and perspective.

In my world, I had heard about it many times. But I had no idea how to do it, nor did I realize the freedom that comes from finally getting there. That is, until I forgave my stepfather who I hated most of my life and into my early 30s. After I forgave him, there was a tremendous release for me. The love that flowed from that forgiveness was beyond words. It was totally unexpected. It was then I learned the extraordinary power of forgiveness.

Forgiveness Comes From the Heart, Not the Mind

So where do we start with forgiveness? First thing is that the act of forgiveness is not grounded in the emotions or intellect. Nope! It is not something you can feel or think about. It is truly from the spirit. It comes from the heart. Not the mind. Even most religions of the world teach that forgiveness is good for the heart and the whole human being.

Forgiveness does not ask us to give the other person a pardon or to excuse their behavior. It does not ask us give up our ethics or our values. Forgiveness is really the means by which we give up the emotional charge that keeps us upset, that keeps us chained to the past. It is something we do to take care of ourselves.

I know from personal experience that it is difficult to forgive someone without keeping some small corner of our hearts where we store our belief that they were wrong and we were right. That typically happens when we try to find a rational reason upon which to base forgiving someone. Yet, there really isn't any. We cannot think our way to forgiveness. Forgiveness truly comes from the heart.

To experiment with the technique of forgiveness, think about an old grievance we have from the past, some sort of resentment, guilt or anger. Or, just some person who we feel has done us wrong. Now, close your eyes and stop reading and just forgive them. Yes, take a moment right now and give it a try. Let it go! See how it feels.

Be Careful to Not Pull Issues Back In

When practicing forgiveness, it is good to stay aware and alert so that we do not pull the issue back in or continue to accumulate new grievances, resentments, guilt or anger.

Sometimes things happen that trigger the issue and we may feel some of the old negative emotions trying to creep back in. When this happens, take a moment to do the forgiveness practice again. Be sure the forgiveness feels complete. Notice the shifts and changes within. This will really make an enormous difference!

Forgiving Ourselves

When we think about the practice of forgiveness, it's easy to think about our past hurts and the people we might want to forgive. As we take the time to practice forgiveness, be sure to forgive the most important person of all, you!

Forgiving ourselves is number one. It is freeing. It will support you in discovering and expressing your REAL self, the REAL you. It gets us past the conditioning.

So, how do we do that?

We forgive ourselves for all our past behaviors and mistakes. We understand that they were only choices we made based on the time, place and circumstances we were engaged in. Allow it to be what it was. It does not add anything to our discovery of who we really are, at our core, to continually blame or chastise ourselves for something from the past that we cannot change.

We can forgive ourselves for not following through on something we started or for hurting someone. We can forgive ourselves for not taking better care of things or for not becoming this or that. We can forgive ourselves for every bad decision we ever made, each and every coulda, shoulda, woulda moment.

Forgive yourself for everything and anything. Maybe one thing at a time. That is the way I did it. I pulled up my guilt, my shame, my bad behavior, my regrets or whatever, and just forgave myself. It really works!

When we practice self-forgiveness, we free ourselves and begin to open up more and more to our trueness, our authentic selves, releasing the guilt of the past. We lose the past and move more fully into self-acceptance.

Losing the Attachment

Having the ability to lose the past is one of the essential keys to becoming more authentic and REAL. It is in losing the past that we can be present, and able to focus our attention forward.

It is not about losing the memories. It is really about losing the *attachment*. Let it all go. It doesn't even exist anymore. There is only *now*, the present moment.

The REAL you is here and now.

In the process of letting go you will lose many things
from the past, but you will find yourself.
Deepak Chopra

*Allowing ourselves to be vulnerable means that we
are no longer defensive about our actions.
We allow them to be what they are.*

Key #3

ALLOW YOURSELF TO BE VULNERABLE

Vulnerability is about showing up and being seen. It's tough to do that when we're terrified about what people might see or think.
Brené Brown

Allowing ourselves to be vulnerable is another key to unlocking the door of discovery and expression of the REAL you.

Let's begin by taking a look at the definition of *vulnerable.* It is always good to see how words are actually defined rather than just what we think we know the word means. Misunderstanding words prevents the truth of the matter from coming into our consciousness.

The Merriam-Webster Dictionary defines vulnerable as *capable of being physically or emotionally wounded; being open to attack or damage.* Wow! You mean there's value in allowing ourselves to be open to attack or damage?

Well, that's not exactly what I'm saying here. Striving to be more authentic has nothing to do with physical attacks or assaults. Although it is certainly a good idea to be aware and alert to our surroundings: physically, energetically and spiritually. What I am referring to here has to do more with our mental state, our emotional reaction and our possible defensiveness in the face of some verbal or emotional attack. Being vulnerable means that we allow ourselves to be who we are without fear of criticism or judgment.

Vulnerability Is a Strength

Vulnerability is a sign of strength, not weakness.
Buddha

Many people think of vulnerability as being a weakness. It is not. It is actually a great strength. Why? Because it gives us the ability to grow, to learn more about ourselves and, among other things, to become less defensive.

Why Are We So Defensive?

In my own journey, I learned about defensiveness when I was in therapy. I was unaware of the concept. Once it became known to me, I found it to be a very significant practice to work on. When I really started paying attention and actually catching myself being defensive, I was so surprised to discover how often I did it. It was so deeply ingrained into my consciousness that it continues to be an ongoing challenge for me, even today. Just as with any deep spiritual work, it is a process.

The dictionary defines defensive as *serving to defend or protect oneself; devoted to resisting or preventing aggression or attack.* The example used in the dictionary to convey defensiveness is: *He became defensive when I brought up his spending habits.*

Defensive behavior is, generally speaking, the need to explain to someone why we did what we did. The truth is we never really have to explain ourselves to anyone, ever! Yet, it seems to be a natural reaction for most of us. Themes of life such as *don't trust strangers, everyone is out to get you, don't let anyone get close to you, people only want to hurt you, everything has to be perfect, YOU have to be perfect, and so on,* have all been conditioned into our monkey minds for a very long time. They make us think we have to protect and defend ourselves.

No Explanation Needed

As we grow in our authenticity, we become more accepting of the fact that we all make mistakes. Not everything is, or is supposed to be, perfect. There are instances where we screw up. Hello being human! Allowing ourselves to be vulnerable means that we are no longer defensive about our actions and allow them to be what they are.

In other words, if someone criticizes or finds fault with something we did, and they confront us about it, instead of defending ourselves, instead of explaining why we did what we did, we just let it slide. We simply say, *Yep, I know* or we say, *That's just the way I do things sometimes,* or *Oops, I made a mistake* or *Thank you for pointing that out.* Another possible response could be to answer the question with a question: *Did you not like the way I did that? What are your concerns?* Or maybe we give no response at all, and just nod or smile. Release it without comment. Let it drop. This is always an interesting response!

The bottom line: We stop defending ourselves. We decide that no explanation is needed. We pull up our confidence and move into self-acceptance. When we respond in such a manner, the criticism, fault finding or blame goes nowhere. Or, it drives the other person crazy. It will be one or the other. The important thing is that we give up the need to explain.

I admit, not being defensive is a tough one. Especially when we first start to work on it. Yet, it is a really good practice to integrate whenever we can. Why? Because it fosters self-acceptance. We choose to accept ourselves, warts and all, with no explanation needed. We are able to let our vulnerability flow without the need to be defensive, because we accept that we are human and that we make mistakes.

Even in a work situation where the boss is not happy and is asking us why we did what we did, we don't need to make excuses and defend ourselves. Simply explain what happened and be open. See it as an opportunity to practice being vulnerable and fostering self-acceptance, and not as an attack that needs to be defended. Accept and allow the possibility that we might have made a mistake or misunderstood something. So what? Does it really matter? Mistakes happen. Nobody is perfect. Perhaps there is even something to learn from the situation.

We are not here to be perfect or to live up to the expectations of others. We are here to grow, to change, to evolve.
To become who we really are.

Have you heard that before? If so, have you integrated it? Do you really believe it? I sure do!

Being Open and Vulnerable

When we are open and vulnerable, we are able to simply admit our mistakes and apologize. We don't have to cover it up and make excuses about why we did what we did. We've learned from the experience. We can ask for forgiveness. There is value in this work: self-acceptance, inner peace and well-being.

Part of becoming who we really are, becoming authentically ourselves, is part and parcel of emotional maturity and spiritual maturity, which we talk about later in the book. That means we know we are okay no matter what is going on. Other people's perspective of us, their opinions about how we do or do not do things, is really none of our business.

Not my circus, not my monkey.
Polish Proverb

250 Ways to Wash the Dishes

In my own life, when I was first married, my husband explained to me that I was doing the dishes wrong. I told him there are at least 250 ways to wash the dishes. There is no right way. This is my way. That is your way. See, just different.

We may have to remind people of this along the way, that there is no right way. It certainly applies to more than dishes. Because we are different people, we were taught differently. What may have been right in our family, or how we were taught, was not necessarily the way they did it in their family, or how they were taught. There is no right way, they are just different.

Sometimes, if you just remind people of this, they get it. They are open to the idea and agree that there is no right way. Some people, on the other hand, will never get it. They are damned and determined that they know the right way to do this or the right way to do that. Our practice, in this case, is to be okay with however they choose to respond.

My Way or the Highway

If we are in a situation where we need to either insist on doing it our way or switch over to doing it their way, remember that our job is to be who we are in our own skin, not to try and live up to their expectations or to do it their "right" way to keep the peace.

Now this doesn't mean that we can't choose to do it their way. That's perfectly fine. It's important to pick our battles. Our job, in this situation, is to remain open and vulnerable and to not close up. We quickly weigh out the situation and then decide the best course of action for ourselves. We choose how we want to respond, rather than letting our buttons be pushed and allowing the monkey mind to run around screeching.

Vulnerability Has Value

The concepts being presented here are designed to offer new ideas and perspectives that can be used shift our view of reality. They give us opportunities to decide how we want to BE in the world. It is up to each of us to work these concepts into our lives, to help us feel better about ourselves as we become more and more authentic. In doing so, we learn that vulnerability has value.

While we want to be more authentic, and more accepting of who we are, we also want to be aware and alert to not let the monkey mind rule the situation. We can always learn new things about ourselves when we remain vulnerable.

When we remain vulnerable, we have the opportunity, the space within, to evaluate what someone is really saying to us. *Does it give us a new perspective on our behavior? Is it something we are not aware of? Is it something we may want to consider changing? Or is that person just being critical or unkind, because that is what they do?* Whatever the case, we want to respond appropriately. We want to be authentic. Just do whatever feels appropriate, from the heart, in that moment.

As we stay vulnerable, catch ourselves and then release the need to defend against anything and everything, we find opportunities to explore our real feelings about what is going on. We can then allow ourselves, with full self-confidence, to truly consider what is being said or what is happening, because we have decided to be vulnerable.

Wear Your Heart on Your Sleeve

Another part of allowing ourselves to be vulnerable is what I call *wearing your heart on your sleeve.* It means that instead of putting a wall or barrier around our hearts to protect them, our hearts are out there in plain view, on our sleeves, for anyone to hit, punch, pet, love, admire, break or whatever.

Wearing our hearts on our sleeves does mean that we might be rejected. *Oh, no!* Or that we could be disliked. *Oh dear, no!* Or disapproved of. *Oh, not that!* Or maybe even misunderstood. *For heaven's sake, please, not that!* Oh, yes!

When we decide to step on the path of wearing our hearts on our sleeves and just be ourselves, no matter what is going on or happening in the moment, we are exercising our vulnerability. And, at the same time, our self-confidence.

What happens in real life is that we may not express our true opinions. We may not say what we really feel or think. We may even disguise our feelings, pretending to feel one thing when we are feeling another. Usually this is out of fear of someone else's opinion. Or their approval or disapproval. Or their dislike of us.

My personal experience falls back on the basic foundation that I was a person who wanted everyone to love her. I had no real sense of myself. My need for love and approval was so great that I was like a chameleon. I had no opinions of my own. I would assume the likes and dislikes of whomever I was with. I went along with whatever was happening. God forbid I would say what I actually thought or felt. I was just too afraid of what others would think of me or of their disapproval if I differed from them. I did not dare to wear my heart on my sleeve.

Vulnerability Is a Strength

Part of wearing our hearts on our sleeve means that we allow our vulnerability to be a strength. We say what we think or feel in this or that situation and let the chips fall where they may.

We may do this in small steps. Start with the safest people first. As we gain confidence in expressing ourselves, we can move it to different parts of our lives.

Modifying our behavior and becoming more and more confident in expressing ourselves is part and parcel of growing into the REAL you.

Lose the Affectations (The What?)

There is a level of civility, of social mores and cultural values that tempers, hopefully, all of our behavior. Affected behavior, when someone demonstrates *affectations*, is when someone acts as if they are somebody other than who they really are. This is typically done in order to impress someone or to alter how others perceive them.

We may sometimes act or pretend like we have more than we do, exaggerate what we have or make up stories about our lives. In other words, pretending we are sophisticated, or too cool, or have way better jobs, or have more money, education, status, friends, boyfriends, girlfriends, whatever, than we do. We are affected.

We may feel that these affectations will help with our social standing or impress the people we want to impress. We may feel that people will think more highly of us. However, more often than not, we find that these affectations don't feel right or don't do what we want them to do. Not only does it create internal friction, but it can also cause us to lose all credibility, being quickly detected by others who have their BS meters turned on. And most everyone really has them turned on nowadays.

Sometimes the use of affectations is another part of the barrier that many of us have erected to keep people from getting too close. They are just one more layer that we use to hide our true selves and to protect us from becoming too vulnerable. To protect us from being hurt or rejected. We allow the monkey mind to think it is protecting us.

Pretending to be something we are not can cause us to lose the person we really are. When we do this, we put a struggle upon ourselves. How can we step into our true, authentic self if we lose ourselves again and again with every affectation?

The bottom line is that the use of affectations truly sets us up for failure, no matter how long we pretend to be something we are not. This is true no matter how big or small the infraction.

Let's face it, pushing ourselves to be someone we're not is not easy. It creates a tension in our bodies that is not good for us. It creates a tension in our soul, too. This is not good for us either.

Now is the time to lose the affectations. Now is the time to make the shift.

Make the Shift

I must admit, this was my forte until I found it harder and harder to keep pretending, being pretentious and affected. I know from experience that at some point we begin to feel anxious. More fear sets in, followed by worry and concern about being found out, caught in the deception. How embarrassing is that? It's not a good feeling.

If we don't consciously make the shift now, lose the affections, we will most likely do it after we get caught in the deception. Or, when we get anxious enough about someone picking up on our pretentions. It will simply become too uncomfortable for us to continue doing it.

Ready, Set, Go!

The good news is that we can begin the shift right here and right now. How? We start by declaring that we are going to lose our pretentions, lose our affectations. We make the commitment to be more honest, from here on out. To wear our heart on our sleeve. To allow ourselves to be more open and vulnerable. Folks can just get over it. We let the chips fall where they may.

The truth is, people will either like us or not like us. When we are being ourselves, at least people will like us or not like us just as we are. Who we *really* are. And if there is an issue, they can just get over it ... or not. It is not our problem. It is between them and their monkey mind.

We can do this! No more pretending. No more exaggerations. No more hiding about what we think or feel. This is part of being honest with ourselves and others and part of being vulnerable.

When we do this, we began to step more into the REAL authentic self. The shift begins. Our self-confidence grows each time we shift a little more.

We do it one step at a time.

As we begin to make changes, it helps to start thinking about and observing certain patterns. *What mannerisms, actions, language, swagger, clothes, do we use to convey how we want others to perceive us? Are we being true to ourselves? Does it feel right?*

In many cases, we are only doing it to obtain the approval of our friends or family. Or so that our peers or business colleagues will accept us.

Falling Into Old Patterns

Our work is to catch ourselves when we fall into our old patterns of pretention or affectation. Remind ourselves that we are in the process of changing it up. Recognize that this is not who we are any longer, that these patterns do not feel right for us anymore. They are not part of who we really are.

Small Changes First

Remember, it is important to make small changes at first. Move on to getting more and more comfortable with being who you really are. Step more and more into confidence. You can do it!

The REAL true you is awesome!

Sometimes You're the Pigeon and Sometimes You're the Statute

Another part of allowing ourselves to become vulnerable is realizing and accepting that sometimes we are the pigeon and sometimes we are the statute. I love that concept! There are many other perspectives on this theme which convey the same concept: *Sometimes you are the dog and sometimes the hydrant; sometimes the hammer and sometimes the nail; sometimes the bug and sometimes the windshield.* All good themes for something that is really just a part of everyday life. Part of accepting what IS.

This concept supports acceptance of our lives no matter what is going on. When we allow ourselves to be vulnerable, we know that things change all the time and sometimes they don't go our way. One of my favorite sayings is, *Oh well.* That concept also flows us right into one of my favorite stories which has turned out to be one of my favorite practices!

I Don't Mind What Happens!

My favorite spiritual practice is based on the story about Jiddu Krishnamurti (1895-1986). He was a philosopher, speaker and writer. He is said to have had no allegiance to any nationality, caste, religion, or philosophy and spent his life travelling the world, speaking to large and small groups and individuals. He wrote many books. Here's the story which was reported most recently in The Guardian magazine in 2013: *Krishnamurti gave countless talks at which he frequently implied that his audience shouldn't be wasting their time listening to spiritual talks. But perhaps the most striking was a 1977 lecture in California. "Part-way through this particular talk," writes Jim Dreaver, who was present, "Krishnamurti suddenly paused, leaned forward and said, almost conspiratorially, 'Do you want to know what my secret is?'* (There are actually several accounts of this event; details vary.) *Krishnamurti rarely spoke in such personal terms, and the audience was electrified, Dreaver recalls. "Almost as though we were one body we sat up ... I could see people all around me lean forward, their ears straining and their mouths slowly opening in hushed anticipation." Then Krishnamurti, "in a soft, almost shy voice, said: 'You see, I don't mind what happens.'"*

Whaaattt??? *"I don't mind what happens."* Wow! I love that!

In other words, he's saying that he is not attached to a specific outcome. He is at peace with whatever happens.

I think this correlates rather nicely with our pigeon and statue analogy. Sometimes we may be the one in charge of providing a situation which changes someone's life or causes them some intense feelings. Being the pigeon, if you will. And sometimes someone is in charge of providing a situation which changes our life or causes us intense feelings. Being the statute, if you will.

Whether the pigeon or the statute, we all have the ability and the choice to remain steady, balanced and not mind what happens.

Choose to Be Steady and Balanced

Often when I share this concept with others, the response is, *But I DO care, I DO mind!* Not minding what happens has nothing to do with whether or not we care. Sure, we can care. We can stand up for things; we can do things, whatever. Not minding what happens has to do with accepting things as they are. We don't resist the reality that is right in front of us. We roll on through, choosing to remain steady and balanced, trusting that All Is Well at the highest level. Why? Because this is what's happening in front of us. It is our reality. And we can know and trust that there is a natural order to everything that is happening, way beyond our human understanding.

The Choice Is Ours

Rather than rolling on through, we can, of course, always choose to be sad, depressed, angry, upset, frustrated or afraid. Or we can choose to say, *Oh, well, I don't mind what happens,* and simply relax into what's up. It is what it is, so to speak.

This practice saves us from so much anger, frustration, tension and anxiety. It is all about relaxing into what is happening, being here now and observing and discerning the forces at play in the Universe.

My friend Cristina and I got to experience this first hand when we were pretty new at our practice of not minding what happens. We were all lined up at our gate at the airport, so excited to be off on a speaking trip together and ready to go. It was then that the announcement came over the loudspeaker – our plane was delayed. We looked at each other and said, *Well, aren't we glad we don't mind what happens?* We both broke out laughing. It was great!

Of course sometimes it is much harder to practice *I don't mind what happens*. In my own life, when my sister died, I found myself feeling that sometimes it's hard not to mind what happens. The bigger picture is, of course, that everything that happens is part of the natural order of things, whether or not we realize it or understand it. There are tough situations that hurt deeply. This does not change the higher perspective that releasing the pain allows us to grow and change and evolve into a more balanced state of being.

It takes practice, for sure, yet we do have that choice. Even for the most challenging things that happen to us, this concept supports our mental, physical and spiritual health. It keeps us as steady and balanced as possible all through our lives.

When things do throw us off balance, and some things may, we have the opportunity to choose to not mind what happens. This allows us to be emotionally vulnerable and to not have our old reactions, conditioning and triggers kick in.

Being Vulnerable Is Courageous

Allowing yourself to be vulnerable is an act of great courage. Why? Because you are not hiding behind a façade to appease others, to protect yourself or to defend yourself. Instead you are merging with your true authentic self and becoming the REAL you.

Wearing our hearts on our sleeves allows more healing than we can yet imagine. It brings our growth to a whole new level. Start with those small steps. Know that there is nothing to defend or protect. It is just the monkey mind that takes command in its attempt to protect us. Tame it, train it and switch to trusting your heart's knowingness, your heart's wisdom, and not the voice in your head. It is then we can appreciate how vulnerability gives us strength, courage and self-confidence. This is one of the keys to becoming who we really are.

Key #4

STOP CARING WHAT OTHERS THINK

To escape criticism do nothing, say nothing, be nothing.
Elbert Hubbard

Another key which unlocks the opportunity to change our lives, and be the REAL you, is to stop caring what others think. We do ourselves a great favor when we learn to not worry about how others perceive us. This, like all the other keys, is best taken one step at a time. Understanding how it affects us and how to change it are important phases in our personal development. So let's look at how this plays out.

Sometimes we will do or not do something we want because we are concerned with what other people think. We hold back. We don't express our opinions. We don't do what we want to do. We don't go where we want to go. We don't wear what we want to wear. This is part and parcel of what we just discussed in the last chapter, allowing ourselves to be vulnerable. It is based on the fact that, in essence, in those instances, we care more about what someone else thinks than our own feelings.

Our Most Important Relationship

One of the benefits of doing this work, that of discovering and expressing who we really are, is that it gives us the opportunity to develop a brand new, wonderful relationship with ourselves. It is important to realize that the most important relationship in the world is the one we have with ourselves. We really cannot help and support others, or be of service to humankind, if we are not taking care of ourselves. We need to understand and accept that we are our most important relationship.

Focus on Ourselves

Our reality is in the process of shifting from an old world to a new world. From an old externally-focused reality to a new internally-focused reality. We are shifting into the New Reality.

In the old world, focusing on ourselves was considered selfish and improper. It was condemned. The value touted in that reality was putting others first, always. In that world, selfishness meant being excessively concerned with oneself to the exclusion and disregard of others.

Now, in the new world, the New Reality, we have a much greater understanding of how important it is make ourselves the most important focus, our most important relationship. To strive to become more authentic, transparent and in integrity with our real feelings and thoughts. To express our true self.

As we shift into the New Reality, we become more conscious of what we are doing, how we are treating ourselves and others and what is happening in our lives. We regularly observe how we are expressing ourselves in the moment. We become more and more aware of what is going on in our daily lives. *Do we like it or not? Do we want to change anything about it?*

Our lives really do reflect how we are treating ourselves. When we affirm that the relationship we have with ourselves is our most important relationship, we feel happier. We make better decisions. We are more authentic. We are more able to be of true service, not just lip service. We understand that we need to take care of ourselves in order to take care of others.

Sometimes old world, old worn out concepts impinge on our beingness, truthfulness and integrity. Therefore, to move beyond and into the New Reality, the new world of being the REAL you, is something that is really worth doing. To take care of ourselves, to be more conscious of whether we wish to allow ourselves to be influenced by others and to grow and evolve by becoming more self-confident and capable.

Other People's Opinions

*Care about what other people think and you will
always be their prisoner.*
Lao Tzu

No matter why we think we do it, at some point we all have based our actions and decisions on what someone else may think of us. What happens? We end up not doing what we want to do because we are afraid of what our friends, family, school mates, workmates, colleagues, and, gads! even sometimes total strangers, will think.

Before I began to really work on myself, in my personal life, I think you can gather that I was not the most confident person.

When I first began to pay attention to and notice how much I let others influence me, it was another big step along the path of discovering myself. When this insight of not caring what others think about me came into my consciousness, I realized deep in my heart that there will always be people who won't like me no matter what I do. That was a big realization. I firmly planted myself in the place of knowing that I would rather have the people that like me, like me for who I truly was.

This does not mean that you completely stop caring about what others think or how they perceive you. It does mean that you decide whose opinion matters, and if and what weight their opinions have on your decision-making. It is beneficial to have a few close people whose opinions you trust to support you. It is wonderful to have those people in your life.

You have no responsibility to live up to what other people think
you ought to accomplish. I have no responsibility to be like they
expect me to be. It's their mistake, not my failing.
Richard P. Feynman

What about other people's opinions? Do they really matter? In the final analysis, probably not. What we wear, how we comb our hair, what music we like, how we express ourselves, how we do this, how we do that, there are lots of opinions out there. And lots and lots of people who think they know the right way for everyone to do everything.

Remember the story of the 250 ways to wash the dishes? These people don't stop themselves from letting us know either. They are always the first to offer their opinions, whether we've asked for them or not. Some folks have probably not done too much introspection. They may not realize yet that everyone is a unique sovereign entity. That everyone is doing what they feel is right for themselves as best they can, whether they are aware of it or not.

Making Decisions

When was the last time we didn't do what we wanted to do because we cared more about what other people would think? It is probably much more frequent than we realize. Part of this process is taking a look see and becoming conscious of when and how we make those decisions. That is the first step. Becoming aware of when and how and who we are allowing to influence us.

Once we become aware, we are then in a position where we can make conscious choices. Our decisions will no longer be based solely upon the influence of others and what others will think of us. That is why awareness is so important.

Of course, it is fine to allow others to have some influence on us when making decisions, as long as we are not doing something just because we feel we have to. Or, out of fear or concern of what someone else might think. We can choose to be influenced by them because we are aware of their influence and it feels like the best course of action. We choose it.

Remember, what others think of us is none of our business. What we think of ourselves IS our business. When we step over ourselves to do the bidding of someone else, we are betraying who we really are. Not so if we think about it and make a clear and deliberate choice.

Social Media Has Changed Everything

Another area this concept plays out in is social media. This arena has become a source of constant anxiety and social pressure for many. Games, Facebook, Instagram, SnapChat, different apps, and so on, all provide an experience of virtual reality that we all live in. Many people are influenced by on-line personalities and profiles that may not even be real human beings.

I was a privacy and information security lawyer for many years. I am amazed at how many people created fake profiles. Why did they do it? It was mainly for the purpose of influencing other people. However, sometimes the purpose was to steal identity, other times to steal information or even to steal money. These kinds of people also create profiles for the purpose of bullying others, to make them feel bad, to make them feel less than. Some use these fake profiles to just get their own anger and venom out at someone safely, without having to confront them personally. People really do respond to and are influenced by these on-line negative energies.

Don't Give It Legs

If you have a negative on-line experience, here is my advice:

First analyze the situation. Is it someone who is real, someone that you know? If so, there are things you can do in that instance. You might be able to have it removed. If it is not someone you know, or if it is anonymous, there really is not much you can do about it. Therefore, if you cannot have it removed, if there is nothing you can do about it, then don't give it legs.

What I mean by *giving it legs* is this: if you begin to respond and defend yourself, the issue gets legs in the sense that it can walk away from you and get all blown out of proportion. You do not know who you are dealing with or what their intention is. It may have nothing to do with you and everything to do with the other person. Defending and protesting only helps the person attacking. They are getting what they want, your attention or the attention of a lot of other people! That may not be at all what you want.

It is true that many people are empowered by the Internet and social media as a means to share their negative opinions about anyone or everyone. Because of the possible anonymity on the Internet, people have no problem being jerks and letting their opinions fly. The pool of negativity has grown larger and deeper. Participate or not, at your choice.

Do keep a level head. Post only things that feel good and bring in positivity. When we stay authentic on-line we build a community of like-minded people who will truly love us for us. If we are mistreated on-line, we do not need to keep them as friends or relations. It is okay to purge your life of toxic personalities no matter where they are, no matter who they are, and that includes our families. That's all part of spiritual and emotional maturity.

Stop Taking Things Personally

As we speak of purging toxic personalities, the other side of the coin is putting ourselves into the place where we step out of the monkey mind and into our Higher Self. When we are dealing with any kind of harsh reality, it is best not to get caught up in it.

Whoa, and how do we do that? How do stop ourselves from getting caught up in it? Well, we have to take a moment to step back, take a breath and gather ourselves.

Don't Take Anything Personally!
Don Miguel Ruiz

When another person projects negative energy onto us, it's time to turn to what Don Miguel Ruiz said in his book, The Four Agreements, *Don't Take Anything Personally!* This applies whether someone comes to us in anger or mean-spiritedness or even if they are just being insensitive or unkind. When we choose to not take it personally, we free ourselves.

Don Miguel Ruiz says that nothing other people do is because of us. It is always because of them, whatever is going on with them.

We All Live in Different Worlds

All people live in their own dream, in their own mind. We are all experiencing completely different worlds, based upon our own unique perspectives.

When we take something personally, we make the assumption that the other person knows what is in our world. They don't! Even when the situation seems so personal, even if others insult us directly, it has nothing to do with US. What is said, what is done, what their opinions are have nothing to do with us. It only has to do with their own mind.

Psychologists Agree

Psychologists are in agreement with the concept about not taking things personally. They add that it makes us easy prey. Easy prey? Why? Because we get hooked so easily into another person's perspective. Then, when we are fed whatever poison they are dishing out, whatever criticism or judgment they are feeding us, we take it personally. We eat it all up and it is not good for us at all. It can actually make us sick!

As we work on the practice of not caring so much what other people think, not caring what they will say if we do this or do that, we are reminded once again to not take things personally. It is helpful to know that we have this psychological support.

How to Stop Taking Things Personally

So how do we stop ourselves from taking things personally?

The first step is to notice when we are doing it. Become aware of our thoughts and feelings after we have been harshly criticized or insulted. *Have we been triggered? Are any buttons pushed?* Notice the behavior of our monkey mind. *What is our monkey mind telling us?* We can ask, *Am I taking this personally?* If the answer is, *Yes,* then it's time to have a little chat with ourselves.

When working with the monkey mind, we can remind ourselves that whatever is going on is going on with them, not us. We recognize and understand that it is truly not about us at all. We don't have to explain this to the other person. We just have to know it and feel it within ourselves.

This practice really works! Try it!

Take Everything With a Grain of Salt

It is true we cannot avoid criticism. We can learn to live with it and not allow it to have such a grip on our lives. We can get to the point where we care so much about ourselves and our ideas that we are not put off by a negative review or opinion, not a critical comment or even a raised eyebrow.

I would imagine that most of us have heard the expression, *Take everything with a grain of salt.* Meaning, don't take everything as being necessarily true or of having value. In this context, it's good to remind ourselves that when we take the opinions of others too much to heart, we can get caught up in the chaos of many differing opinions about how life should be lived. When we do this, it really pulls us out of who we are. It sways us into other people's worlds, viewpoints and perspectives which may be very dissimilar from our own.

Since there are as many perspectives on how life can be lived as there are human beings, it is important to remain open-minded about all of it. At the same time, we need to be able to detach ourselves from everything else and stand in our own truth.

The truth is, people really only speak from their own experience and understanding. Each of our paths are completely different. Remember the old adage and take everything with a grain of salt. Set yourself free!

Be True to Ourselves

There is freedom that comes from being true to ourselves and not caring so much about what other people think.

Never underestimate the beautiful power and freedom that washes over us when we commit to being true to ourselves. That is the focus and purpose of this work. It challenges us to keep going deeper and deeper.

When we stop letting fear and anxiety prevent us from sharing ourselves, our creativity, our desires or from being the person we are, we step into the freedom to choose how and who we want to be at any given moment.

How do we do that?

One way is to stop asking people what they think of us or what they think of our ideas. Especially people who we know do not have our best interests at heart. Or, those who are predominantly critical, pessimistic or unhappy. We know their comments might reflect their negative and, possibly, unhealthy perspective.

This whole practice is, in essence, a desensitizing of ourselves. We recognize that everyone has their own opinions, and that's that. We don't take it personally. We recognize and value our own perspectives and ideas. We realize that we do not need to please everyone.

It is one thing to say we don't need to please everyone and it is another to fully acknowledge and accept it. There are really only two options here: either we accept it or we don't. If we choose to not accept it then we will continue to experience the pain of trying to please everyone all the time. If we choose to accept it, on the other hand, this moves us beyond to freedom. Freedom to be who we really are!

Speaking Our Truth

People are judging us all the time and there is nothing we can do about it. We're doing some of the same, eh? Lots of judging going on with our monkey minds. The thing to remember is that we don't need people to like us. It is the relationship we have with ourselves that matters most. It is our own self-acceptance that matters. And it is *our* people who matter. Those we choose. Our tribe, if you will.

In order to become who we really are, changing ourselves and ultimately the world, it is important to remove and overcome the obstacles of feeling disliked, being lonely or feeling like a loser. The shift from caring what others think to not caring is more than just developing thick skin. It is really about becoming free.

Part of that freedom comes with speaking our truth. We speak it when in conversation with friends, family and coworkers. Standing firm in our true beliefs and opinions supports us.

We may want to back down if we are contradicted in some way. However, when we speak our truth, we may find that even a little dissent in the conversation actually keeps things interesting. If we are open and light hearted, speaking our truth doesn't necessarily lead to conflict or being disliked.

When we stay true to ourselves, even when faced with opinions that are different from our own, we'll gain more confidence in ourselves and in our beliefs. Others tend to appreciate folks who are being real and it may give them the opportunity to be more real themselves.

Live in the Present Moment

Be Here Now.
Ram Dass

Being more present in the moment also supports our freedom. This is particularly applicable when we are in conversation with other people. Being in the here and now prevents us from being distracted or appearing disinterested. We are able to really listen to what the other person is saying. Being present is not thinking about what we are going to say next or making judgments on what the other person is saying. If we find ourselves there, stop and bring the focus back to being present. Just listening.

When we are being present, our anxieties and concerns about what others might think tends to fall away. We feel better and more confident in ourselves.

Follow Your Heart

Remember, it's normal to care about what other people think. We certainly care about what people we love and respect think of us. And we might even care about what strangers think of us. That's perfectly normal. The practice of not caring what other people think simply means that we honor our own perspectives and make decisions that come from our own ideas and from our own hearts. We choose not to be influenced by what other people might think. We are confident within ourselves.

Our confidence offers us a choice to decide who and how and when we allow ourselves to be influenced. If we find we are being influenced by fear or anxiety or by wanting others to like us, this it the best time to check in with ourselves and decide how to honor ourselves best. To speak our truth, to not join in, to not opine, to not involve ourselves. The choice is really ours.

Whenever we are following our heart, when we are present, when we are inspired and following our passion, we are able to develop the confidence within ourselves to stop caring what others think. It's possible that we are just marching to the beat of a different drummer. Most of the time that's true. In fact, we may find that our greatest achievements come from the sound of our very own drumbeat. Honor it!

The practice of not caring about what other people think simply means that we are no longer outer directed by the opinions of others. We don't take things personally and we make choices based on what feels right for us, in the now moment. We start caring more about what WE think. We start taking better care of ourselves and the relationship we have with ourselves. We step more fully into becoming who we really are.

Be who you are and say what you feel, because those who mind don't matter and those who matter don't mind.
Dr. Seuss

Key #5

BE OPEN AND HONEST

Be honest in your life, it creates positive energy.
Fathima Bibi Joosab

Being open and honest with yourself and others is the final key to unlocking the door to discovering and expressing the REAL you. Oh boy, this is a good one!

This practice is about exploring our own self-honesty, the deep inner truth about ourselves *with* ourselves. It is also about how we openly and honestly express ourselves to others.

Create a Deeper Connection

When we choose to become more open and honest in our lives, we give ourselves the opportunity to create a deeper connection with ourselves. It is this relationship that is the most important of all. The relationship we have with ourselves. Self to self.

Once we have begun the exploration of our depths, we are in a better position to decide how much of ourselves we want to share openly with others, and how much we want to keep to ourselves. We get to decide. The choice is ours. The important thing is being honest with ourselves.

Armed With Self-Confidence

If we have been following this book chapter by chapter, key by key, then so far we have worked on accepting ourselves, losing the past and allowing ourselves to be vulnerable. We have worked to stop caring so much about what other people think, releasing the need to let others influence us unless we choose to let them do so. By doing this work, by exploring these keys, we are now in a stronger position, armed with a more stable foundation of self-confidence.

The next step is to be open and honest with ourselves and others.

Where do we begin?

Old World vs. New World

The first step to becoming open and honest is to decide if being open and honest with ourselves and others has value for us. *Is it something we care about? What value does it have? Any? How would this thing called being open and honest be expressed?*

In the old world, the old 3D reality, honesty and truthfulness were not necessarily held in high regard. Generally it was better to be closed and protective; don't talk to strangers, don't make eye contact with others, don't smile, and certainly, do not engage strangers in any way. Take no risks. We still see this today. The old world of duality was based on fear, lack and mistrust. Separation. The *other* is bad, we are good.

In the new world, our new internally-focused reality, the attribute of honesty is honored and appreciated. Truthfulness is valued. It is about being open and transparent. It is about being real. When we are real, it inspires others to be real too. We free everyone up.

In the new world, the New Reality, we smile at someone and they smile back. There is a human connection. Simple. Easy. If we smile at someone and they look away or don't smile back, we can presume they are either not present or they simply don't want to connect, for whatever reason. In some cases, it may be that they are just surprised that we are smiling at them. Their monkey mind could be thinking, *What's up with that person?* Or, maybe they think the smile was intended for someone behind them. In any case, we just roll on – continuing to smile and be happy, not at all concerned about why they didn't smile back. Not minding what happens.

Smiling, being friendly, open and accessible comes from doing the work. It is ours to do, or, of course, not do. It's our choice.

What Does Being Open Really Mean?

First let's look at being *open*. What does it really mean? There are lots definitions for it, and I'm sure we all pretty much know what it is or have a feeling for it. However I want to be clear on what I am referring to here. The kind of open or openness I speak of is about number eleven on the Merriam-Webster's dictionary list of definitions of open. It says, *characterized by ready accessibility and usually a generous attitude ... willing to hear and consider or to accept and deal with ... free from reserve or pretense ... accessible to the influx of new factors.* This accessibility, generosity, listening and accepting others and ourselves without pretense, and allowing new and different perspectives, is what we are talking about.

It does not mean that everything comes at once. When we step into the desire to be open, the whole world becomes new. Our consciousness, our lives, our relationships all change because we allow the new, different and the questionable to be included in our perspective.

So, what about being honest?

What Does Being Honest Really Mean?

The honesty I refer to in this chapter is about being honest with ourselves. What does being honest really mean? First let's look and see how the word *honest* is defined. The Merriam-Webster Dictionary defines the word honest as being *without fraud or deception; genuine, real.* This definition fits what we are talking about here. When we come to terms with it, being honest means no fooling ourselves or rationalizing what we do. We need to be genuine and real. This is done inside ourselves. It does not have to be shared with anyone.

Some people choose to identify the odd things they do as being quirky or eccentric. They simply accept those quirks as part of their our own humanness, their own imperfections. After all, we all have them. Right? This is perfectly fine as long as we are being truly honest with ourselves.

Being honest about our imperfections supports our personal, spiritual and professional development and evolution. In doing the work to become more open and honest, true and authentic, there are a couple more things for us to consider.

Our lives improve only when we take chances and the first and most difficult risk we can take is to be honest with ourselves.
Walter Anderson

Being Honest With Ourselves Can Be Difficult

Being honest with ourselves can be difficult. Why is that? Because, in essence, we are confronting the raw truth about ourselves. We are looking closely at our actions, behavior, thoughts and feelings. We are confronting the real stuff, the part of us that we don't usually show to other people. The stuff we hide away from even ourselves.

We all have concerns about our flaws. Who doesn't? We are ashamed or insecure about an aspect of ourselves. Who isn't? This is where we start. We begin by taking an honest look within.

Here is a good example of not showing the raw truth to other people: I read about a woman who, while stepping into being honest with herself, shared that she would wolf down an entire McDonald's meal on her way home from work. She would even dispose of the trash before she got home, ridding herself of the evidence. Then, once she got home, she would sit down and eat another meal with her family. Up until that point she had not shared that truth with anyone before, nor had she been honest with herself about her behavior. I am sure we each have some of our own stories to tell.

Does it matter that she did not share the raw truth with other people? Does being honest mean we need to confess all of our flaws and shortcomings to the world? No, of course not. What matters is that we are honest with ourselves.

The power in self-honesty is choice.
We get to choose. In the present moment.

Being honest with ourselves also means that we acknowledge when we need to change our behavior. We acknowledge when we are doing something that does not support who we are and what we value. This is the part of discovery that can be the most difficult.

If we are not used to being honest with ourselves, we might be surprised to find out how challenging it is to confront those issues within. Why? Because we have hidden so many things from ourselves for years. We rationalize our behavior. We make excuses for ourselves. We do not own up to our actions. That is not being honest.

The Practice of Being Open and Honest

Now let's take a look at the practice of being open and honest. This includes speaking our truth, telling the truth and forgiveness.

Start Slow

First, know it's okay to go slow. In fact, if we move too fast, the monkey mind will hide everything from us. We will not discover or move into the ability to root out causes and conditioning. We do not have to do everything all at once. We can do it in bits and pieces. It is much easier in small chunks. It took us all our lives to get to this point. By going slowly we can get used to it. Over time it becomes a practice that we can integrate. We check in with ourselves all along the way while we are living our lives. It truly is a lifelong process.

Your Truth vs. *the* Truth

The first step along this path is to notice that speaking *your* truth and telling *the* truth may be two different things. People go on and on about this at great length ... truth versus reality, *your* truth versus *the* truth. This is a very philosophical discussion. It all depends on one's perspective. Suffice it to say that it may be of benefit to think on these things and to distinguish *your* truth versus *the* truth.

Many folks seem to fly over this concept. There are objective facts and then there is the Truth, with a capital T. There are subjective feelings, thoughts, ideas, beliefs, opinions that are ours and ours alone, maybe shared, maybe not, that are *our* truth.

The point is, one of the steps along the path of being open and honest, and practicing honesty and integrity, is to understand this difference.

Everyone is entitled to his own opinion,
but not to his own facts.
Senator Daniel Patrick Moynihan

Part of being open and honest is making sure we speak our truth. We may find ourselves not saying what we really mean or feel or even think on a given subject. Being completely honest with ourselves and others is an important aspect of living life, of mastering life. It supports us as we move into being more and more our true authentic selves.

It is work to discover who we really are. That work pays off with big dividends as we live it and learn to love and appreciate our lives. Speaking our truth is one of those important steps!

No more beating around the bush, no more half-truths or white lies, particularly to save someone's feelings.

Being Critical vs. Being Honest

This does not mean, however, that being unkind is productive in any way. For instance if we point out someone else's flaws or make judgments on how they look or how they comb their hair, or about the state of their health or anything like that. That is not what is meant by being honest or speaking our truth. Be sure to distinguish between being critical and being honest.

When we listen to ourselves, when we are aware, we can watch the way we say things. I have heard some pretty awful, mean and rude things said when people were "just being honest." We must understand that standing in judgment, criticizing, disapproving or making wrong is not being honest. It is often mean-spirited, even if or especially if it is self-directed. We are frequently far more unkind to ourselves than we would ever consider being to anyone else.

It makes me think of the old Biblical admonition about *picking the speck of sawdust in someone else's eye while paying no attention to the plank in your own eye.* It is always good to be conscious of and pick our timing intuitively, from the heart. This is especially true if we know it is something that would cause an emotional reaction or potentially hurt someone else's feelings, or cause them to get defensive. Confrontation and truth-speaking are not the same thing.

Saying Yes When We Really Want to Say No

Speaking our truth also covers those situations where we find ourselves constantly saying *yes* when we really want to say *no*.

No is a complete sentence. We can learn to stop doing what we do not want to do. Again, it takes practice. If we allow someone to make us feel like we are not good enough, not smart enough, not good looking enough or if we are losing our sense of self, then it is time to speak up.

With our new sense of self-confidence, and having worked the practices, we can do it without fear. We just have to do it and then do it again. Then do it again. Soon it becomes easier and easier.

Honesty Sets Us Free

Another aspect of this is talking straight about what is really going on with us. If we are holding anything in or if we have something to share with others, particularly with someone who is close to us, we have to step into our true, authentic selves and do that. It is so, so good for us.

When we speak our truth, when we are authentically ourselves, there is an openness that comes from our heart that releases us and allows more and more love and support to come in.

Honestly, speaking the truth is liberating! So do speak up about what you want, what you feel and what you need.

Many of us are deceiving ourselves, in any number of ways, every day. We may or may not even be aware of it. As we step into being open and honest, we step into releasing the oppressive burden of lying to ourselves. This causes shame and guilt. Honesty really sets us free.

Being entirely honest with oneself is a good exercise.
Sigmund Freud

Peeling Back the Layers

It is not until we really get honest with ourselves that we realize the work is internal, not external. It is about peeling the layers off to get to our true core.

How do we do that?

We explore. We ask ourselves questions. We write them down.

For example, *What am I doing with X behavior? What don't I want my best friend to know about me? Why? Do I lie to myself? What about ...? What is my next step?*

As we write, some interesting things may come up which help. Keep writing. Keep exploring. Do the work.

Seeking Outside Assistance

If we struggle getting to our own core, if we aren't able to find our own truth, we can always seek help. Using outside assistance can be of value. There are professionals we can ask to help us if we have difficulty going deeper. Or, we can ask people who are close to us, who care about us.

If we do choose outside help, know that the monkey mind may have something to say about it. There may be some resistance. If so, rest assured that if we shut off the monkey mind on this subject, and honor our own needs, we can easily move through any resistance that might come up.

Our purpose is to set ourselves free. This is sometimes best done with an objective person who has real listening skills. Find a counselor, life coach, therapist, friend or partner who can help support you along the way as you do this work. Just something to consider.

Forgive Yourself and Others

One of the reasons people lie to themselves and others is to escape the consequences. Maybe they did something wrong, or thought they did. Maybe they are embarrassed for making a mistake. Maybe they did not live up to their responsibilities.

Forgiving ourselves is an important step that allows us to move forward from the painful feelings we may have about our own mistakes, failings or misdeeds of the past. Forgiving ourselves may feel strange. Yet, self-forgiveness is a very, very powerful tool of liberation.

When we take ownership of our problems or failings or mistakes or misdeeds, we are ready to move our life forward. We forgive ourselves. We can then go into our future in a very positive way. Step by step, of course, but this is a big step. We can practice this one daily.

The practice of forgiveness allows us to unbury and unburden ourselves from past actions, events, grievances, perceived insults or disrespect. Moving these boulders out of our lives really frees us up. So many times our perspective on something is colored by the actions, events or people in our life that have wronged us in some way. We may have past traumas that we have not dealt with completely. We do not know what to do with that feeling of being a victim. Now is the time to bring these things up. Stop thinking about them. Get them out of the mind and into the ethers where they can be transmuted and no longer exist. Release them and become free!

Forgiveness is not an occasional act;
it is a permanent attitude.
Martin Luther King, Jr.

Forgiveness Comes From Deep Within

The act of forgiveness is really a spiritual initiative rather than a rational experience. It is from the spirit. There really isn't any rational reason to forgive. Releasing any lingering remorse, guilt or anger through reasoning is impossible.

When we finally realize that forgiving ourselves and others will burst open the flow of love into our lives, we become capable of forgiving from a place deep within us. It is from this deep place within us that the love flows.

No matter what it is or how horrendous it is, forgiveness from that place deep within releases our soul on its further journey. When forgiveness is real and true and from the heart, it is over and done with. We just don't relate to it anymore. It's like a button that is flattened and doesn't work any longer.

Forgiveness Releases the Old

When we make forgiveness our daily practice we release old grievances, resentments, guilt or anger when they come up. We also want to be very conscious not to continue accumulating new grievances, resentments, guilt or anger. How do we do that? We let it go. Forgive and let it go.

When I am doing my own forgiveness work, I take a leaf from a religious notebook. It is written that Jesus said on the cross: *Father, forgive them, for they don't know what they are doing.* This is what I say to myself when I am forgiving others: They don't know what they are doing. It's not personal. They just don't know. I forgive them. This forgiveness practice helps me not accumulate that which blocks the flow of love in my life.

People who mistreat or hurt others, whether done on purpose or inadvertently, are lacking the consciousness of living in harmony and in the love vibration. As we birth the New Reality, with the understanding that we are all One, we come to comprehend that forgiveness is essential.

People can do the most unbelievably heinous things, and they are responsible for their own actions. Forgiveness is the key to not accumulating internal pain, particularly for the actions of others. We forgive them, and in doing so we free ourselves.

Forgiveness is also a key to the release of the superficiality, the untruthfulness, the deceit, the little white lies, the affectations, the pretending that prevents us from being open and honest with ourselves and others. Practicing forgiveness is about putting one foot in front of the other.

The true path of forgiveness is one of forgiving everyone and everything that you meet. This is the process that will set us free to live in love and be who we truly are. Becoming free of the past every step of the way.

Relax Into the Work

While this work can be tiring and hard, requiring persistent and dedicated effort, the rewards are unbelievable. The freedom that comes is amazing. Keep writing. Relax into the work. Keep it at the forefront of the mind. Ask questions. Admit mistakes. Be straightforward.

What if we sometimes goof? So what. Hello! Human here!

Pay attention to thoughts, emotions and feelings. Be aware in each moment. Remind yourself that being open and honest is important and takes practice. Accent the positive and take time to reflect.

Being open and honest with ourselves may not be easy. Yet, if we remember to laugh with and at ourselves, we can make it through. Practice forgiveness. Let go of old grievances. Speak the truth. Be real. Be open. Be honest. These are essential keys to becoming who we really are.

Our past does not have to define our present.
Our failings do not have to define our future.

In Conclusion: The Five Keys to Unlocking the REAL You

A very little key will open a very heavy door.
Charles Dickens

Now that we have explored all five keys to unlocking the REAL you, we have opened the door to a new kind of freedom. There is no turning back now! We have a greater sense of empowerment. A greater sense of purpose. A greater sense of who we really are.

When working with these keys, we can also see why it has been so difficult for us to be authentic. We can see why we thought we were being ourselves when we weren't. Not our true, authentic selves. Now we know what steps to take to free ourselves so that we can become who we really are.

The five keys are:

1. Accept Yourself

2. Lose the Past

3. Allow Yourself to be Vulnerable

4. Stop Caring What Others Think

5. Be Open and Honest

Even though each of the five keys provides a different focus or perspective for us to practice and learn from, we can also see how interrelated they all are. They all encourage us to become more authentic and real.

The five keys collectively teach us to become more aware of our internal thought processes, the way we feel, what we say and what we do. To make conscious choices. To choose what we want to keep and what to release. To choose how we want to respond. To be open to our own self- discovery. To nurture and take better care of ourselves. To be more honest about how we feel. To speak our truth. To free ourselves from our conditioning so that we may become more and more who we really are.

Becoming the REAL You Is a Process

We have learned from The Five Keys that becoming the REAL you is a process. It challenges us to become more and more authentic on a daily basis. It may not always be easy. Sometimes it will be hard. Yet it will always bring us to a deeper connection with ourselves, our most important relationship.

Emotional and Spiritual Maturity

As we integrate The Five Keys more fully into our lives, we will discover that it brings us to a new level of being. This new level of being is the beginning of the re- creation process. We become more authentic and true. We become more loving. We become more honest with ourselves and others. We speak the truth. We are more open to new ideas and information. We forgive those who we feel have done us wrong, and we forgive ourselves for wrongs we may have committed. It all works!

This new level of being is called emotional and spiritual maturity. And, yes, it is a good thing! I will be covering it in detail starting with the next chapter.

The REAL You

In the meantime, as we continue to work with and explore The Five Keys, know that these keys will continue to guide us. If we continue this work, they will remind us again and again what is most important ... the relationship we have with ourselves. Being true to ourselves.

The Five Keys all work together as one, to point us to a certain place in our being. That place is deep in the center of our true natures, our true selves. This is where the truth of who we really are comes from. It comes from the heart.

Ultimately, working with The Five Keys can help us to develop a stronger sense of who we really are. They can lead us to a broader and more expansive version of ourselves, and help us to awaken to a greater sense of personal freedom and empowerment.

These are the keys that can help unlock the doors to the REAL you!

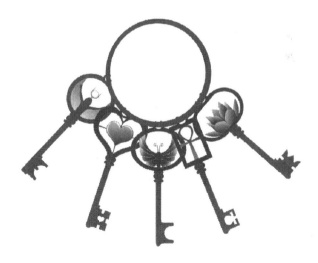

Anyone who has ever looked inside knows that the work takes persistence. It takes desire. It takes heart!

Emotional Maturity

*You may find that your greatest achievements come from
the sound of your very own drumbeat.*

Emotional Maturity

Part of spiritual and emotional maturity is recognizing that it's
not like you're going to try to fix yourself and become
a different person. You remain the same person,
but you become awakened.
Jack Kornfield

There are many aspects to emotional maturity, just as there are many aspects to our emotions. I want to share just a few here. Ones I found were important in my personal development. They really helped me along the way. So first, let's explore what emotional maturity is. Then we can get into a few specifics.

What Is Emotional Maturity?

Emotional maturity refers to our ability to understand and manage our emotions. Being emotionally mature means we think before we act on our emotions. Or before we choose to suppress them. As with the recurring theme throughout this book, we do have a choice in everything we do, whether we realize it or not.

Emotional Intelligence (EI) and Emotional Quotient (EQ)

The concept of emotional maturity goes hand in hand with the important discussion, often found in the professional world, of Emotional Intelligence (EI) and Emotional Quotient (EQ). We have all heard of the Intelligence Quotient (IQ) which measures intelligence. Well, the EI and EQ have to do with how capable a person is of recognizing their own emotions, therefore, making them more able to understand the emotions of others.

The term Emotional Intelligence was coined by Peter Salovey and John D. Mayer in 1990. They described it as *a form of social intelligence that involves the ability to monitor one's own and others' feelings and emotions, to discriminate among them, and to use this information to guide one's thinking and action.*

Daniel Goleman became aware of the research work of Salovey and Mayer and wrote the book, <u>Emotional Intelligence</u>. Daniel Goleman was a writer for the *New York Times*, specializing in brain and behavior research. He trained as a psychologist at Harvard.

Goleman described emotionally intelligent people as those with these four characteristics:

1. They were good at understanding their own emotions, self-awareness.

2. They were good at managing their emotions, self-management.

3. They were empathetic to the emotional drives of other people, social awareness.

4. They were good at handling other people's emotions, social skills.

Emotional Maturity Is Not Intellectual

Emotional maturity is the application of that EI or EQ in real life. It is not intellectual. It is really awareness that exists beyond the intellect. It's like the difference between knowledge and wisdom.

Emotional intelligence is about knowing what your emotions and feelings really are. Emotional maturity is about wisely applying that knowledge.

There are tests that can actually measure emotional intelligence. Emotional maturity, on the other hand, is tested in the real world, in daily life. Together with spiritual maturity, emotional maturity enables us to really create the life we desire.

There are different attributes of emotional maturity. I have chosen my favorites, the ones that I have found to be most supportive to the quality of life. So, do read on!

Responsibility

Look at the word responsibility 'response-ability' the ability to choose your response. Highly proactive people recognize that responsibility. They do not blame circumstances, conditions or conditioning for their behavior. Their behavior is a product of their own conscious choice, based on values, rather than a product of their conditions, based on feeling.
Stephen R. Covey

When I talk about responsibility and emotional maturity, I'm talking about taking responsibility for ourselves. Oh, say it isn't so! Many equate responsibility with control. However, one of the greatest illusions in our world is the illusion of control. I think most of us know and understand that. Yet we continually try to control people, places, things, timing, situations. When we are emotionally mature, we bust the illusion that we have any real control and take up the gauntlet of responsibility.

Responsibility? Yes. I think we all have an idea or concept of what responsibility means. However, it may mean different things to different people. Most of us think we are responsible people. We go to work, we pay our bills, we pay our taxes, we take care of our pets, we take care of our children. This is what responsibility is all about, right? Well, sure. Yet, it is only partially right. It is right in the old world of duality sense.

In the old world, the old reality, society saw a responsible person as a value. Someone who minded their manners, respected their elders, controlled any kind of emotional outburst, and pretty much put on a mask of pretension. That was a responsible person.

That certainly is still true. Those of us on the path of exploring who we are, looking ever deeper within ourselves, learning more and more about who we are, see being responsible as a value. We also realize it is way more than that.

What Is Responsibility?

So, what really is the meaning of *responsibility?* There are actually a few different definitions. The Google definition says that it is, *the state or fact of having a duty to deal with something or having control over someone.* Interesting, control over someone. Really?

The Merriam-Webster Dictionary defines responsibility as, *the state of being the person who caused something to happen and/or a duty or task you are required or expected to do and something that you should do because it is morally right, legally required, etc.*

Now those definitions can apply to our emotional maturity but most point back to the old reality. What you *should* do. What is *required* to be done. In the new world, the New Reality, I would ask that we contemplate what Stephen Covey's quote says, that responsibility is the *ability to choose your response.* The ability to respond.

Responding vs. Reacting

The spiritual or personal development path teaches that having the ability to respond is separate from the wisdom that needs to be attached to that response. In other words, to *respond* is more of a thoughtful, conscious, activity. The other side is to *react.* Most reactions come from the monkey mind, from fear, anxiety, panic, conditioning, doubt, habit or from concern about what someone will think. Generally it is from something other than thoughtful consideration of what is at play in front of us.

Blaming Others

One example of reacting is to immediately search for someone to blame when something goes wrong. *Do we look to blame others? Do we believe others deliberately go out of their way to make our lives miserable or unhappy?* Well, maybe they do sometimes. No, no, just kidding. Although certainly sometimes it seems like the actions of others are directed at us or they cause us problems or make life difficult.

Do you remember the practice of working on not taking anything personally? When we give conscious thought to this process, we know there is so much going on at any given time that blaming others is just the easy way out. We see it all the time, do we not? *It's their fault! Whose fault is it?* Who cares?!

Fault finding and blaming others is not emotional maturity. Life happens. Stuff happens. People make mistakes. When we accept responsibility, and consciously choose how we want to respond, that is emotional maturity.

There is one more thing to say in this blaming others context. Accepting responsibility for our deeds and actions means that we understand that many of the circumstances that exist in our lives are the result of the decisions and choices we have made along the way. If things go wrong, and they do sometimes, we do not want to be blaming others. It is not emotionally mature.

In addition, when we are exercising emotional maturity, we do not blame ourselves, either. We accept responsibility for our deeds, actions, decisions, choices and whatever. That is not the same as taking the blame. Certainly, if we deliberately did something wrong, we own up to it. Everyone makes mistakes. It's human. Sometimes it's awful and embarrassing, yet owning up to it is simply that. We take responsibility. It does not mean that we are necessarily to blame.

Responsibility and blame do not go together.

Blame is one of those useless actions Wayne Dyer talks about in his book, _Your Erroneous Zones_. He says blame is a waste of time. That taking responsibility is very empowering. Why? Because we realize we can make better decisions and take better actions because we know mistakes may happen. We take the risk. We accept the responsibility. That way, we don't just sit around wallowing in misery or complaining about others or making excuses for ourselves.

> _Most people do not really want freedom because freedom_
> _involves responsibility and most people are_
> _frightened of responsibility._
> Sigmund Freud

So, as we contemplate our level of understanding of how or even if we are responsible people, it becomes part of the process. It is about staying conscious about our level of responsibility as we walk our path. _Are we being it? Are we practicing responding rather than reacting?_

There is drama, drama, drama everywhere. This gives us our best opportunity to practice, practice, practice being responsible by being a force for change amidst the dramatic goings on of the world.

We Are Responsible for Everything in Our Lives

Part of being responsible is knowing, at the deepest level, that we are responsible for everything in our lives. Whoa! Whaaat??? There is real learning, growth, and practice when we step into that understanding. This deeper wisdom begins to take us into the realm of spiritual maturity, which will be introduced more fully in the next section.

I know that the concept of being responsible for everything in our lives sounds off the charts. However, Eastern traditions have taught for millennia that true spirituality is being aware and conscious that we are interconnected with everything and everyone else. We are One Being. Even our smallest thought, word and action has a real effect throughout the Universe.

I know that may sound crazy, yet it's like the pebble thrown in the pond. The ripples move and merge with one another and create new ones along the way. Everything and everyone is inextricably interconnected.

With this understanding of Oneness comes the realization that we are, in fact, responsible for everything we think, everything we say and everything we do. We understand that we are really and truly responsible for ourselves.

And from there, we can expand our understanding even further. We begin to realize that we are essentially responsible for everyone and everything else and the entire cosmos. Whoa Nelly! Let's take this a step at a time, shall we?!

In today's highly interdependent world, individuals and nations can no longer resolve many of their problems by themselves. We need one another. We must therefore develop a sense of universal responsibility ... It is our collective and individual responsibility to protect and nurture the global family, to support its weaker members and to preserve and tend to the environment in which we all live.
Dalai Lama

Flexibility

Life isn't about surviving the storm;
it's about learning how to dance in the rain.
Anonymous

When I talk about flexibility in relation to emotional maturity, I'm talking about being flexible in mind, body and spirit. Yes, all of it. Learning to be more flexible in our lives is a most important function. The emotional maturity of flexibility, like responsibility, morphs into spiritual maturity too. Being flexible, actually doing it, is indeed both a spiritual and emotional practice.

Being flexible is the most efficient way of living our lives once we learn that it is about adapting to the world around us.

Incorporate Being Flexible Into Your Life

Incorporate flexibility, really being flexible, into your life. With our feet planted in our foundation of self-confidence, we step more and more into our true authentic selves. This involves integrating flexibility. Flexibility is all about going with the flow, bending with the breeze.

Using the analogy of a tree, with its roots firmly planted in the soil, it is still flexible and can bend and sway with the highest of winds. The trees that are not able to flex in the wind, or adapt to the changing conditions, either get uprooted or are snapped off.

The shifting of zones between duality, the old world, and the greatly expanding New Reality, the new world, are stirring up lots of changing conditions for everyone. Maybe even some high winds in our lives. Therefore, setting our intentions and then integrating our spiritual selves into the world we want to see, really works. It works because, as Mahatma Gandhi said: *We must be the change we want to see in the world!*

There are several levels of definitions in the English language for *flexibility* and each one applies to what we are talking about here. First it is defined as *being capable of being bent or flexed.* I am sure we can feel what this means. It is about being pliable, not being rigid, not being so fixed on what it is we expect, want, desire that we cannot move when things change. That's how folks break, snap.

Bend With the Breezes, Winds, Whatever Comes

If we add to that concept the *capability of being bent repeatedly without injury or damage,* I am sure we can feel that too. At least at a gut or intuitional level. When it seems like things keep piling on and piling on and piling on, many folks get confused, depressed, break into drugs or use alcohol to deaden the feelings of overwhelm.

I have heard many people say when one thing after another kept happening: *What else can go wrong?* or *What more can happen?* Sure enough, something else does go wrong or more unpleasantness happens. Therefore, it's wise not to say things like that. Just don't go there. We are truly powerful manifestors, powerful creators, and we must be careful what we think and say!

Thoughts Become Things ... Choose the Good Ones! ®
Mike Dooley

Be Responsive to Change

Being flexible is also about being responsive to change, being adaptable. Fits right in with responsibility, doesn't it? All of this fits into our spiritual practice. The ability to be flexible, to be pliable, to be strong in the face of daunting situations and to be adaptable keeps us steadfast in the truth of who we are. It supports our authenticity, our trueness and our heartfelt knowing that All Really Is Well.

Part and parcel to this is knowing and noticing that time, as we know it, is changing. People tend to want to slow it down. It only seems to keep accelerating. Really, our consciousness has shifted.

With that comes an understanding that there is clock time, *Chronos*, which gets you where you want to be at a given time and there is *Kairos*, which measures moments, not seconds. Kairos measures the right moment, the opportune moment, the perfect moment, and is more flexible and malleable. Consider flexibility in your relationship with time.

There Is Only Now

From an emotional and spiritual maturity perspective, there really is only Now. Understanding this truth gives us the opportunity to compress or expand time. We can choose to *be here now* at any time. Feeling crazy about time? Choose Now. Think about it.

As we show what flexibility means in our world to others, we support others in their processes. We broaden our perspective so that we can experience any person, situation or project with a view not previously obtainable. We don't have to say anything, just be and act flexible.

Adjust and Adapt

Life is filled with change. Nothing stays the same. Conditions and circumstances are constantly in flux. Each and every situation or circumstance that we encounter is unique. Therefore, there is no reason to whimper or complain about what is going on with life and its burdens. Life is just doing what life does. When one is emotionally mature, we simply adjust and adapt as needed using emotional and spiritual maturity. Our spiritual tools keep the monkey mind managed.

When we manage the monkey mind, we are then able to keep ourselves in a steady state. We can be calm, handling what needs to be handled. We can fall apart later if we have to. Flexibility and adaptability provide an inner peace that supports us as we go through life's challenges. We are able to adapt to the unfamiliar, unpredictable and dynamic circumstances that go on in our lives. No rigidity, no snapping or breaking in the winds.

Changing Your Mind

*I feel I change my mind all the time. And I sort of think that's your
responsibility as a person, a human being, is to constantly
be updating your positions on as many things as possible.
And if you don't contradict yourself on a regular basis,
then you're not thinking.*
Malcolm Gladwell

For some reason people talk about the idea of changing your mind in a derogatory manner, as if there is something wrong with it. In the old world one was admonished, You don't change horses in mid-stream. Then the new world reality came along and said: You do if the horse is going the wrong way!

Women have been made fun of for years, centuries even, because there has been this idea that women always change their minds about everything. This new world idea must have been something women have known forever, I guess. My point is the same as Malcolm Gladwell's point, that there is absolutely nothing wrong with changing our minds. It fits right in with being flexible and, in my opinion, intelligent.

We make up our very own beliefs and ideas about the way things are based on what we know. It behooves us to change that up when we are presented with additional information. It is not only emotionally and spiritually mature, it is the smart thing to do. It can be amazing how in the face of solid factual evidence, folks can still hold onto their conditioned beliefs or what someone else has told them is true.

The measure of intelligence is the ability to change.
Albert Einstein

Shifting Thoughts and Behaviors

Being flexible allows us to change our minds and integrate our personal development tools. These tools also support the ability to be tolerant of different ideas and different ways of doing things. Flexibility enhances the capacity to shift thoughts and behaviors. When we know that we can change our mind about anything, we are not rigid in our thinking. We can move through life at an easier pace. When we have no expectations about the situation we are in, we can be open to whatever comes and adjust along the way. Being flexible also means we are not attached to the outcome. Flexibility is an aspect of emotional maturity that goes hand-in-hand with spiritual maturity.

Non-Judgment

The ability to observe without evaluating is the
highest form of intelligence.
Jiddu Krishnamurti

One of the attitudes of emotionally mature people is the practice of non-judgment. *Certainly, you may say, but Darity, we have to make judgments all the time.* That is correct. However, it is a matter of perspective. *Are we being aware, discerning? Or are we being critical, making a judgment?* It is important to distinguish judgment from discernment.

Some people who choose to work on being non-judgmental think that it means looking at everything through the eyes of goodness. That they need to always be nice and see the good in everything. To be positive no matter what. This outlook makes one unable to spot the objective differences in people's abilities, talents, gifts, situations and conditions. Put differently, by desiring to be non-judgmental, these folks may not be using their natural ability to be attentive and discerning.

Non-judgment is one thing and discernment is another. Although acknowledging the relative value of one thing against the other is important in making human decisions in life, it is also important to remember that non-judgment has a spiritual perspective that transcends both the physical and emotional levels.

A New Way of Life

First let's talk about non-judgment as a new way of life. A new way of life? Yes!

Emotionally mature people understand that the practice of exercising non-judgment brings more expansiveness and inner peace into our lives. Judging people or situations as right or wrong, good or bad is the way of the old reality. We are crossing the bridge to the New Reality, one of internal focus and Oneness.

Non-judgment allows us the opportunity to really, really engage in true compassion and understanding. It allows us to support all of our fellow living creatures.

The Path of Non-Judgment

It is true that non-judgment is not an easy path to follow. Indeed, it is one of the more difficult ones because of the profuse amount of conditioning provided by our parents, educators, friends, life, etc. It is only when we stop to look at it closely that we realize the truth of the matter that we have been conditioned to judge everything and everyone around us, constantly.

Here's a story from my personal life to illustrate this point. Every year on my birthday, I have asked Spirit for a guiding path to focus on and work on throughout the year. Some years ago I was given the path to learn how to exercise non-judgment. I remember thinking, *What's that?* I told a friend of mine about this path. She laughed out loud at the very idea. *You can't do that!* She said, *How the heck can you do that? Everything is a judgment one way or the other.* Being an attorney at the time, I thought that seemed right. *How the heck am I going to do that?* You know what, over the course of that year I learned the truth of the matter. I began to understand the difference between judgment, discernment and observation.

I found for myself, through non-judgment, a much higher level of acceptance for *what is*, more than I ever had before. Instead of judging everything in my life as good or bad or right or wrong or whatever, I learned about and experienced the joy that comes from releasing judgment. It is through using the concepts of discernment, perception and observation that we can begin to change up our need to judge everything and just allow it to be what it is. Not the easiest thing, I can assure you, but it works!

Judgment Defined

In order to better understanding what *judgment* really is, let's look at the definition from the Merriam-Webster Dictionary. It says judgment is, *an opinion or decision that is based on careful thought.* In my experience, the types of judgment we are talking about here are not about what color to wear or which car to buy or any number of mundane decisions or judgments we make in our daily life. It is about shifting our consciousness from the mundane to the growing understanding that the old world is over.

We now, as global citizens wish to bring love, peace, compassion, understanding and tolerance into our daily lives and the lives of others. Judgment, in the old world context, is about the black or white, good or bad, right or wrong, good or evil, duality based concept of judgment. The new is about accepting what is.

Discernment vs. Judgment

Finally, let's talk about discernment. What is discernment? It is *perception in the absence of judgment.*

In other words, whatever is, is.

Without the ability to discern, we could not get through life. This is how we make our everyday decisions. What to wear, how long to sleep, where to work, what to have for lunch, a million things.

Having discernment means that we can discern someone's actions without making a judgment about it. We can value everyone as being equally worthy, even as we recognize differences in their abilities.

Being judgmental, on the other hand, has to do with whether or not they are worthy in the eye of the person doing the judging. *Can you look at a homeless person with compassion rather than judgment? Or do we think to ourselves, What a waste! Get a job!*

A person who is being judgmental can sometimes go well beyond simply discerning differences in people. They can make inferences and draw conclusions about the other person's overall worthiness. To a judgmental person, for instance, a bad cook is considered to be inferior not just on the aspect of cooking, but also on the more fundamental aspect of being human. They are judged to be unworthy and inferior as a human being because they cannot cook.

Judging is acting on limited knowledge.
Learn the art of observing without evaluating.
Pushpa Rana

We are taught from an early age what is right and what is wrong. What is good and what is bad. Those precepts follow us all our lives. Being emotionally mature and exercising non-judgment allows for the discernment of a wide variety of lifestyles. We allow people and situations to be what they are, and to do what they do.

Everyone is a sovereign being on their own soul journey. Not our circus, not our monkey. None of our business, other than to love, have compassion and accept.

The integration of non-judgment is to watch ourselves and catch ourselves every time we start thinking judgmentally. What people say, what people do, who they are, what they look like, they are just being themselves, doing their thing. No judgment necessary. Practice. Practice. Practice.

No one knows how much you know until
they know how much you care.
Theodore Roosevelt

Characteristics of Emotional Maturity

There are many different perspectives on the attributes and characteristics of what constitutes emotional maturity. Some folks say when we are emotionally mature we have achieved true adulthood. (Holy Moly, I'm not sure I'm ready for that!)

Here is some food for thought. These are the characteristics of Emotional Maturity as described by the *Associates for Personal and Family Counseling*:

The emotionally mature person:

- Accepts criticism gratefully, being honestly glad for an opportunity to improve.

- Does not indulge in self-pity. Begins to feel the laws of compensation operating in all life.

- Does not expect special consideration from anyone.

- Meets emergencies with poise.

- Feelings are not easily hurt.

- Accepts the responsibility of their own acts without trying to alibi.

- Has outgrown the all or nothing state. Recognizes that no person or situation is wholly good or wholly bad and begins to appreciate the Golden Mean[1].

- Is not impatient with unreasonable delays. Has learned that they are not the arbiter of the universe and that they must often adjust to other people and their convenience.

- Is a good loser. Can endure defeat and disappointment without whining or complaining.

- Does not worry unduly about things that cannot be helped.

- Is not given to boasting or showing off in socially unacceptable ways.

- Is honestly glad when others enjoy success or good fortune. Has outgrown envy and jealously.

- Is open-minded enough to listen thoughtfully to the opinions of others.

- Is not a chronic faultfinder.

- Plans things in advance rather than trusting to the inspiration of the moment.

[1] The Golden Mean, from Ancient Greek philosophy, is the desirable middle between two extremes, one of excess and the other of deficiency.

*Allow the truth of who you really are
to run your life.*

Spiritual Maturity

If we let it, change awakens us
to the sacred process that it is.

Spiritual Maturity

Comfort replaces insecurity when one realizes that the most important goal has already been accomplished. That goal is to be on the road of spiritual dedication. Spiritual development is not an accomplishment but a way of life. It is an orientation that brings its own rewards and what is important is the direction of one's motives.
David R. Hawkins, M.D., Ph.d

There are many wonderful experiences that come into our lives once we begin down the path of self-discovery and expressing our true authentic selves. Of doing the work. What is the value of this? My answer would be spiritual maturity and emotional maturity.

Both spiritual and emotional maturity tend to move our lives into a different perspective. A much more expansive, open, enticing and challenging way of living. We can fit it all in along the way, if we have the desire. It is a true form of life mastery.

The value that comes from being ourselves is the attainment of emotional maturity together with spiritual maturity. Both of these together enhance the ability to manage our lives as we encounter all of life's many experiences. We've already covered emotional maturity. Now let's talk about what spiritual maturity is.

What Is Spiritual Maturity?

In order to understand what spiritual maturity is, let's first take a look at spirituality.

Spirituality is neither a belief system nor an ideology. It is the surrender of one's ego to the infinite wisdom and knowledge that is Cosmic Consciousness. The All That Is! This is how I define spirituality. We can, of course, modify or change the words *Cosmic Consciousness* to our *higher selves, God, Allah, Yahweh, the Universe* whatever word or name you chose to describe that energy.

I like this definition because it is sufficiently broad. If someone has a particular religion or belief structure, or even if they have none, they are able to feel that spirituality can fit within the parameters of their life.

We all have an ego. That is for sure! The shift to the New Reality is about an internal focus. This combines with the understanding that humanity and all life on the planet, in the solar system, in the Universe, in the Multiverses are all One. In my opinion there is a fundamental connection with a higher power. Some define that power as ourselves, some as God, some the Universe, whatever or however we describe it.

It is not necessary to believe in God or really in anything beyond ourselves. Belief is personal and subjective and based on choice. Many find that their beliefs expand their relationship to self and others.

In one sense, our whole life is a progression of 'knowings.'
Each one is necessary and, if you are looking for Grace,
each one has to be surrendered, sometimes more
than once to get to the next stage.
Susan Bliss Pearce

Spiritual Maturity Allows Creative Power to Flow

Spiritual maturity is based on consciously allowing the creative power, God, our Higher Self, whatever, to work through our lives in such a way that happiness, fulfillment and what makes us feel good comes from inside ourselves. That is where we are doing the work. Yes? It's an inside job.

In my personal world, I came to the conclusion long ago that I am responsible for my own happiness. I am in charge of that and take full responsibility for it. Nobody and nothing can make me happy, only I can do that. That was a big step for me.

Another big step for me was to consciously take a look at what practices people considered spiritual. The more I explored, the more I realized they were part and parcel of stepping into my true authentic self, becoming the REAL me. There is the monkey mind work and the soul or spirit work, both of which absolutely go hand in hand together. One giving spiritual maturity and the other emotional maturity. Spiritual practices support us on the path of life. Many are difficult to integrate.

Some of those spiritual practices are: compassion, trust, love, fearlessness, awareness and consciousness, understanding and tolerance, humility, forgiveness, integrity, and non-attachment. *Can you feel some of them? All of them?*

Non-attachment is a big step both spiritually and emotionally. Let's take a look at it.

Non-Attachment

The root of suffering is attachment.
Buddha

What is non-attachment? Spiritual literature says non-attachment is a goal, a path to enlightenment. It goes with the Krishnamurti perspective, *I don't mind what happens*, that we talked about earlier.

When we set our feelings on a certain situation turning out a certain way, that is attachment to a particular outcome. *We don't want it to rain on our picnic. We want someone we like to notice us. We want our favorite sports team to win. We want our flight to leave on time.* These are examples of emotional attachment. We want everything to turn out the way we want, otherwise we will be very disappointed. We will not be happy unless the outcome matches our hopes or expectations. That is attachment.

Now, a lot of people tend to think that the spiritual practice of non-attachment is about being emotionally cold and unfeeling. Not so. Non-attachment is quite the opposite. Some people, when they think of attachment, think of their kids or their wife or husband, *I'm certainly attached to them.* That's for sure and there is no negative connotation in that. We are all attached to certain things.

The practice of non-attachment is not so much about what we hold onto, as what holds on to us. It is part of understanding the impermanence of everything. Essentially, attachment is the unwillingness to accept what is.

Attachment is the origin, the root of suffering; hence it is the cause of suffering. Yet, there is no need to sell everything and become monks or nuns to practice non-attachment. We simply need to understand the vital importance of acceptance and letting go. As we release attachment, we are more able to step into compassion and tolerance.
Dalai Lama

When we release emotional attachment, we allow it to be what it is. This enables us to live fully and lovingly. We are no longer dependent upon people, things or thoughts in order to feel good. In other words, it does not have to devastate us if what we are wanting does not go our way or if someone does not do what we want them to do. We are just not attached anymore.

The attachment is what creates the suffering: anger, frustration, sadness, disappointment, heartache. The monkey mind views it as a loss. Being super attached to things and people can lead to physical illness or fatigue. It can create setbacks and reduce our vitality. We want to feel good, right? Not sad or angry that things didn't go as we wanted. A person striving to be spiritually mature is relatively free of attachment.

Our Emotions Show Us Where the Work Is

When we find ourselves disappointed, angry, frustrated, sad, whatever, by someone or something not going the way we want, this shows us where our work is. We can then process letting go of our emotional attachment to the outcome. To *not mind what happens*. To use the mantra of *Love and Trust*. To continually remind ourselves to stay present, to set our goals and to not be emotionally dependent upon them.

In my personal experience, when something does not work as I had hoped or wanted, the monkey mind jumps right in with disappointment, sadness, anger, frustration, whatever. It tries to take me down the *Ain't it awful?* road. This is where the work to train the monkey mind comes into play. When I am able to stop it before it gets a hold of me, and answer it with, *I don't mind what happens,* or *Love and Trust,* or *This is the way it is supposed to be,* then I can bring myself back to a place of inner peace.

The Practice of Non-Attachment

Imagine what it would be like to truly not mind what happens. It's raining on the day we planned a picnic. *Oh well. Guess we will either picnic inside or do our picnic another day.* Or *I'm going to stay inside and watch the rain, or go out and dance in it! It's all good.* This is non-attachment to outcome. It takes a while to get used to. That's why we call it a practice. With practice, the results are incredibly freeing. It's amazing to be fine with whatever is. Check it out in your own life, and notice the results.

When we first start to practice non-attachment, it may help to start with something kind of small and easy. Be open to the opportunities. It's okay to start by feeling disappointment and upset. The practice is to first notice the feelings, and then to change your mind. So, notice the feelings, then let go of the attachment. See what happens. It can be surprisingly fun!

Compassion and Tolerance

Compassion and tolerance are not a sign of weakness,
but a sign of strength.
Dalai Lama

Spiritual maturity also includes compassion and tolerance. It is my understanding that scientists have started to actually map out the biological basis of compassion, suggesting that it has a very deep evolutionary purpose.

The research which Dacher Keltner talks about in his essay on *The Compassionate Instinct* has shown some remarkable physiological results. The research shows that when we feel compassion, our heart rate slows down. In addition, the brain secretes the bonding hormone oxytocin. And regions of the brain linked to empathy, caregiving and feelings of pleasure light up. Amazing!

It is good for humans to experience compassion.

What Is Compassion and Tolerance?

Compassion is defined as *sympathetic consciousness of others' distress together with a desire to alleviate it*. It defines tolerance as *sympathy or indulgence for beliefs or practices differing from or conflicting with one's own*.

Both tolerance and compassion support our journey through life. Particularly in dealing with the rest of humanity. Know that most everyone is suffering in some way. It's true. This understanding is a spiritually mature perspective. Why is that? Because compassion represents the healing energy for us as well as for others. When we accept everyone's frailties and shortcomings with compassion and tolerance, we provide a sense of love and a positive flow of creative force that supports humanity. It is about committing ourselves with unconditional love to help ourselves and others become whole.

Exercising compassion allows us to be very gentle. To be patient. To take it easy. It is loving and healing to provide compassion as well as tolerance. It renews our sprit.

When we observe everything with love and compassion, we allow ourselves to feel the reality of the human condition, especially for those who are downtrodden, struggling in life or even those who are just not the nicest folks out there.

Neither compassion nor tolerance excuse anyone's behavior; they merely provide us a method to step out of judgment. Accept others and recognize the perfection of the soul and spirit in everyone.

The Practice of Compassion and Tolerance

While a lot of folks dismiss the attributes of compassion and tolerance as just touchy-feely irrational behavior, the scientific research, as well as our very own heart space, is showing us the importance of compassion and tolerance as a spiritual practice. A spiritually mature person incorporates compassion and tolerance as part of their life practice. It is good for us and it is good for the world.

Part of spiritual maturity and the exercise of compassion and tolerance is to understand that everyone is on their own soul journey. Everyone is driving their own bus through life. We only drive our own. We may share the ride, yet there is only one in the driver's seat. It is about releasing the illusion of control and acknowledging the sovereignty of each and every being.

Compassion and tolerance allow us to accept and bless others on their journey. To love them and understand they are here to make their own choices about everything.

This practice flows right into another spiritually mature idea, the perspective of humility.

Humility

Instead of putting others in their place,
put yourself in their place.
Amish Proverb

Humility is an interesting concept. The words *humble* and *humility* have lots of charge on them. This is because of the connotations that have been linked with them from thousands of years of use.

In the past, people who were humble or exhibited any form of humility were generally looked down upon. The perspective of folks looking down was that they were superior, dominant and powerful. Those others, not so much. This feeling of superiority also fit a few of the foundations of the old reality which is based on fear, lack and mistrust.

What Is Humility?

From the perspective of the old reality, humility would be defined as *lowliness, meekness or submissiveness,* as in a humble birth, humble beginnings, not worth much, poor. It was about knowing your place, not reaching out or up to things above ones station in life. In other words, not getting too uppity. Humility has also been described as lacking self-confidence, being timid, having low opinions of ourselves.

In our new world, however, our new reality, having a balanced, steady and inner focus gives evolving humans a brand new perspective on humility. This new perspective is that humility really takes on the qualities or conditions of modesty, selflessness, respectfulness and egolessness.

Modesty and Respectfulness

I think we probably get a feeling of what *modesty* is. The sense may come from old world thinking because it is defined simply as *having an unassuming or moderate estimation of one's abilities.*

We probably get a feeling for *respectfulness*, too. That one seems easy, whether it be old world or new world, it is about *giving particular attention or holding in high or special regard.* I think respect and being respectful is about consideration or being considerate. Then, oh yes, there is egolessness.

Egolessness vs. Egotism

Now, *egolessness* is generally described as not having an inflated view of one's self-importance and brings in a feeling of Oneness. A feeling of being inextricably woven into the very fabric of our surroundings or environment. Selflessness is a similar concept.

To better understand the idea of egolessness, let's consider the opposite. The opposite of egolessness is *egotism.* Egotism is *a heightened sense of self-worth or sense of one's own importance.* Whether we are important is not relevant. We are all important in our own way. That's not the point. We can be important and yet still exercise humility or egolessness. We can, of course, always choose to exercise egotism, if that's how we choose to be in the world.

Humility also goes hand in hand with self-confidence. Egotism is not humility or self-confidence. Egotism can thwart our desire to bring the energies of love, compassion, tolerance, support and understanding to the Earth.

Humility and self-confidence really go together. They can be expressed at the same time and really are a part of our new lives, our new stories ... moving us along the path of aligning ourselves more and more to be our true selves.

A New Definition of Humility

Let's contemplate a new definition of humility. Understand that humility is really about modesty, selflessness, respectfulness and egolessness. Humility also includes self-understanding, awareness, openness and perspective.

Exercising humility as we shift from the old world, the old culture to the new world, the new culture, will provide an effectiveness to our lives that is different than what we have ever experienced before. Contemplate and explore this new concept of humility. If it rings true, update the concept.

Humility awakens us to greater, vaster perspectives of who we really are. This allows us greater introspection, going deeper to learn more and to tap into our intuition, our inherent wisdom.

Introspection

Knowing yourself is the beginning of all wisdom.
Aristotle

Introspection is another tool of the spiritually mature person. The process of introspection includes the concepts of going within, tapping into our intuition, using our inherent wisdom and learning about ourselves.

Introspection is more than just looking inside to see what is going on with us. Introspection allows us to explore more deeply who we really are. It helps us to gain a better understanding of our true self.

Introspection is the exploration, discovery, expression and then the wisdom that comes from that exploration and discovery.

Let's take a look at the definition of *introspection*. The Merriam-Webster Dictionary defines introspection as, *a reflective looking inward: an examination of one's own thoughts and feelings.* While basically this is true, introspection is more than just a passive, reflective looking inward. There are deeper concepts to consider. One is *going within* and another is *intuition.*

Going Within

The basic concept of introspection is that of going within. This becomes important when we consider how much of our energy is outward bound. We pretty much live our lives through thought, through the monkey mind, through that world out there.

We find that spiritual maturity brings with it the awareness that there really are times when we need to refill our batteries, take a break from the world, step away from all the drama that goes on day in and day out. We absolutely need to spend some time focused on our inner reality. What that means is putting ourselves into a different mindset than usual, in spite of what is going on out there in our lives. How do we do that? We turn our attention inward as often as we can.

True Power is within, and it is available now.
Eckhart Tolle

The Inner Senses

One of the first things we can learn, when we look inward, is that there are inner as well as outer senses. The inner senses are sometimes expressed as: the inner sight of light, the in ner sound of celestial harmony, the inner feelings of spaciousness and the inner connection to stillness. There are many resources which talk about these concepts in depth. These inner senses deserve our attention and exercise as much as our outer senses. Many folks are unaware that they even exist.

Quieting the Mind

The process of learning to quiet the mind so you can go and be within yourself is an interesting phenomenon. Some people have practiced and are able to just drop right into that place. Others struggle to shut off the ego driven monkey mind. It really does take practice.

In my own experience, when I was working on learning how to quiet my mind, I remember hearing: *Just let the thoughts pass on through like leaves on a flowing body of water or like fall leaves falling from a tree.* That was always difficult for me. What I found worked for me was focusing on my breath.

Breath in ... out ... in ... out ... in ... out.

This did stop the mind which supported me in beginning to learn how to quiet my mind.

When we quiet our minds we find great opportunities to connect with the underlying stillness that lies beneath everything. When we can touch that stillness, that space between thoughts, that space between words, we are strengthening our inner senses, our inner awareness. This helps us in the outer world as much as it does in exploring our inner world.

Through the practice of introspection, quieting the mind and going deep within, exploring our inner world, we have an opportunity to expand our consciousness. Some may call it God Consciousness, Christ Consciousness, Cosmic Consciousness. No matter what we call it, no matter what label we put on it, it truly becomes accessible and available to us, and is an element of our spiritual maturity.

Intuition

A quiet mind is able to hear intuition over fear.
Anonymous

We just talked about going within by quieting the mind as part of spiritual maturity. Why do we need to quiet the mind? To do our internal exploration. In doing so, we may discover that internal exploration brings us the understanding that our intuition, our sixth sense, comes from within. Honoring and using our intuition is an important element of introspection and, therefore, spiritual maturity.

Some people do not believe that there really is such a thing as intuition. It is by taking the time to go within, by introspecting, by listening more closely to our inner voice, that we can truly begin to experience our own intuition. We discover that it is available to all of us. Once we have experienced it, we can then develop the ability to use it more and more in our daily lives.

Acknowledging, learning, trusting and further developing our intuition is a part of grounding and expanding ourselves as we become more real and more authentic. As we become who we really are.

Acknowledge Intuition

In order to understand a bit more about our intuition, the first step is acknowledgement. So, let's stop and think about what intuition is to us.

Intuition. *We know we have it, right? Are we in touch with it? Do we know what it is? Is it just something we listen to occasionally? Only when it is really loud or strong? Or, is it a tool we use in our life practices all along the way?*

We probably have some idea about intuition, some sense of it. We might have spoken of it as a gut reaction or a hunch or a vibe. It is kind of amorphous, this thing called intuition. We may think of it as a feeling, a sensation, a reaction, yet it really is way more than that.

What Is Intuition?

The next step is knowing and understanding what *intuition* really is. It is defined in the dictionary as *direct perception of truth, fact, etc. independent of any reasoning powers.* In other words, we all have the ability to acquire knowledge without the use of reason, without the use of our mind. Intuition comes from a Latin word which loosely translated means *to look within* or *to contemplate.*

*Intuition is that directly perceiving faculty of the soul which at once knows the truth about anything. Unless you have the power of intuition, you cannot possibly know Truth. **It is the knowing power of the soul without the help of the senses or the mind.** (emphasis mine) Intuition can give you knowledge about things which your senses and understanding can never give. Intuition does not depend upon any outside data whatsoever.*
Paramahansa Yogananda

Beautifully said ... *the knowing power of the soul.* Wow!

So, okay, now we know what intuition really is. It is knowledge without the help of the mind or the five senses.

We may have just thought it was some feeling we got once in a while, or something to be used occasionally, if we were even in touch with it at all. A lot of people just blow it off or are afraid of it. Some people are not sure what it is or how it works or why it works or what it has to do with anything.

For the last umpteen millennia we have been a mind-dominated world: *the voice of reason, thinking things through, never trust anything that cannot be proven without empirical evidence, if it cannot be seen, tasted, felt, smelled or heard, it does not exist.* Well, that is just plainly incorrect. Most people know they get hunches. They just don't know what they are, nor do they believe in trusting that soul knowledge.

Spiritual maturity includes recognizing our own intuition and acknowledging the importance of trusting it as we live our lives.

Turn Up the Volume

So let's answer the question: *How important is intuition in our daily lives?*

Well, the truth is, it is actually quite significant to those who want to be authentic, when we want to be REAL. We use it much more than we are conscious of. As we step more and more into our spiritual maturity, we want to make sure that we turn up the volume on our intuition.

How do we turn up the volume? We begin by listening. Deeply, strongly, trustingly. Learn to honor that experience. Anytime there is a decision to be made, we can weigh the pros and cons in our minds all day long and maybe come up with a well thought out decision. However, it is our intuition which really and truly controls the ability to make the right decision.

Developing Intuition

The next step is to develop our intuition, our sixth sense. We have talked about learning how to quiet the mind. We use our common sense and do some daily introspection, learning to trust what comes up. By calmly reasoning with and quieting ourselves, we create our own ability to perceive everything within, as well as without.

The left-brain analytical function loses its appeal as we step into becoming who we really are. We discover that who we are comes from within, to be and express our authentic selves. It is not the age of reason any longer. We are beginning a different time here on Earth. Our intuitive, creative energies are awakening and are eagerly awaiting assignment. Developing and using our intuition will break us out of the constant energy of thought. It moves us into our creative intuitional sense of what is going on. It serves us every step of the way and, as with everything, it is just a matter of practice.

We develop it by tapping into our intuition more and more. We learn to trust it. We understand that our intuition guides our reason. We are able to bring ourselves into calmness, our steady state, and allow our sixth sense, that *knowing power of the soul,* to come through and support us in every decision. Every move and every step we take is guided and supported by our intuition, as we move more and more into our authenticity.

Authenticity

You are the most interesting person you know.
You are the greatest love of your life.
Cristina Smith

So far, in our exploration of spiritual maturity, we have covered the attributes of non-attachment, humility, compassion, tolerance, intuition and introspection. It is time to add the attribution of authenticity and integrity.

You may recall that both of these attributes are part and parcel of each of the five keys to discovering and expressing who we really are.

Authenticity and integrity are greatly needed in our world right now. First, let's talk about authenticity.

What Is Authenticity?

Many talk the talk. Not everyone walks the walk. Everyone is a sovereign being, doing what they do, being who they are. We can all discern if someone is or is not being authentic. That is part of trusting our intuition.

Let's look at how the word *authentic* is defined in the dictionary. It gives us a foundation upon which to build our understanding of our objective to be authentic.

The Merriam-Webster Dictionary defines the word authenticity as the *quality of being authentic* and defines authentic as *real or genuine, true and accurate.* It comes from a Greek word meaning *to master* and before that a Sanskrit word meaning *he gains.* It would seem then that the general meaning, for our purposes here, is being real and genuine, true and accurate, being true to ourselves and who we are.

Being Authentic

What is it to be authentic? When we think about it, we realize that all of our personalities are different. *Who are we at our core level? How do we express ourselves? Are we open, closed, introvert, extrovert, humorous or serious?*

Being authentic is really just stepping up to the plate. We drop all the pretenses, all the affectations and discard what we think is necessarily proper in a particular circumstance. We discard what our conditioning or monkey mind says. We move more and more into expressing the true authentic self that we are. What we really feel, or think or want to do. It's basically about not pretending anymore and just doing what feels right from the heart.

Being authentic involves working on grounding ourselves and our visions. It means being flexible as we walk along our path. It is about learning how to stand in our own convictions and to contemplate at a much deeper level all that is really going on. We can choose to diverge from our usual patterns and move to being authentic in the moment.

Only the truth of who you are, if realized will set you free.
Eckhart Tolle

In the above quote by Eckhart Tolle, the words, *if realized* are the most important part. Between the dictionary definition and

Eckhart Tolle's quote we can know the direction of the work of authenticity. It revolves around working on any blocks or mental structures that continue to hamper us from being and expressing our true, authentic selves, the REAL you. We are able to tap into the pure consciousness that we are.

We drop the pretentions, protections and affectations. We allow ourselves to be vulnerable. We step out with our real self hanging out.

First Fear, Then Confidence

When we step out in authenticity, two things happen. First comes fear and then confidence.

First, fear, especially in the beginning, because we are frightened of what someone might think.

Then comes confidence and satisfaction. Why? Because when we grow up, when we become emotionally and spiritually mature, we know, first, that we are not in the world to live up to anyone else's expectations, right? Second, when we are emotionally mature we know that there will be people who like us and those who do not like us. We really don't need to try to be anything other than our real selves to other people. We discussed all this earlier in the book.

Being Authentic in Our Communities

When allowing ourselves to be authentic, we also need to be mindful of the fact that we have communities that we live in. These include our global community, our national community and our very own local community, our personal tribe.

If we really want people to be able to hear what we have to say in our communities, we need to not only be authentic in expressing ourselves, but at the same time we have to be conscious of the needs of others. Most people expect some type of conformity to community norms. More so in a business situation or structure. You can still be true to yourself without feeling like you have given up something, so long as you are conscious of the choices you are making about being yourself.

In my own experience, when I was a practicing attorney, I had to dress up a lot. I felt it was appropriate so that people would not be paying attention to what I was wearing or what I looked like. They would be able to listen to me and interact with me without that type of superficial distraction. I was still me, the true authentic me. Just because we may choose to dress in ways that are similar to our peers, instead of dressing however we want, this does not mean we are like them. Yet, it totally facilitates more effective communication.

At the same time, it is always good to stay aware and alert. When people tell you to *just be yourself*, there may tend to be some judgment and reaction to one just being themselves. What it means, generally, is to just relax and get along with everyone.

Being authentic is being real no matter our situation, no matter how we are dressed, or where we are. It is about expressing who we are in full consciousness. Allowing ourselves the heart space to know that we are fine no matter who or what is happening. This is part of spiritual maturity.

Integrity

Integrity is choosing courage over comfort; choosing what is right over what is fun, fast or easy; and choosing to practice our values rather than simply professing them.
Brené Brown

Integrity is another attribute of spiritual maturity. Integrity may mean different things to different people. Again, let's look to the dictionary definition to begin our journey of understanding what *integrity* really is. We can see how to integrate it further into the depths of our steps to spiritual maturity. Let's see if the definition moves us in the right direction at a spiritual level as well as at mind, body and energetic levels.

Dictionary.com defines the word *integrity* in three different ways.

First, it is defined as an *adherence to moral and ethical principles; soundness of moral character; honesty.* Sounds good! Second definition is *the state of being whole, entire, or undiminished.* With the example of *preserving the integrity of the empire.* Nice! And, lastly, *a sound, unimpaired, or perfect condition,* such as how we would describe *the integrity of a ship's hull as being important for its seaworthiness.* Wow, moral character, being whole and in sound condition.

Those definitions ring true for a solid understanding of the word integrity. They represent the concept and application of integrity to our lives.

Integrity in the New Reality

I would like to add a fourth definition. Integrity, in the New Reality, means *to live our lives in congruence with our values.* That means we are congruent in mind, body and spirit. That means we are living our truth. That means we are doing the work, the processing and spiritual development, to bring our lives into a state of integrity. It is about true authenticity. Integrity and authenticity go together.

And remember, above all, it is an inside job!

Understanding Our Values

In order to live in integrity, we must understand what our values are. We worked on that earlier in this book. The exploration of our values is not a difficult task yet it does require our commitment to introspection. See how it all goes together? It is an inside job. We have to do the inner work.

For those wanting to expand their consciousness, it might seem easier to just read a book, sit in a lecture, or watch a YouTube video rather than do deep inner work. Unfortunately, that's not how it works. No easy solutions. No quick fixes. It's an inside job. It is all about us. We have to be the ones to do it.

The attributes of spiritual maturity include unconditional love, awareness, consciousness, compassion, purpose, appreciation, fearlessness, responsibility and self-esteem. Notice that these are all areas that determine our values, the qualities we want in our life. What those values are and how they are reflected is the exercise of our integrity.

Living Life Congruently

Being in integrity means living our lives congruently. Congruent generally translates to *harmonious*. This gives us the opportunity to bring more soundness of moral character and honesty into our lives. When we bring more integrity into our lives we end up telling the truth at a new level, with compassion and without fear of what others think. That is amazing growth. We can share our truth, our highest values, in a heartfelt, loving and understanding way without fear or concern of reactions.

As we grow and change and become more and more congruent, we become more and more authentic. We know that congruency flows out into the world, out onto a global scene. Knowing that and bringing more integrity into our lives supports us as we walk our path in life. Not a bad thing, right?

Integrity is not just about telling the truth. It is not just about being a good person. It is also about integrating our values so that we are living in the truth of who we are. To take it a step further, when talking about spiritual maturity, it's also about feeling and connecting with deeper levels of understanding within ourselves. We know that what we know about ourselves expands. We are more than just our ego, more than just our monkey mind or our personality. We are not even these bags of skin we live in. We know we are the consciousness behind and within all of that.

Our Behavior Congruent With Our Values

Consciousness enables the content of our lives to be what we want it to be. Our integrity facilitates it. We contemplate and meditate upon the expressions of ourselves. That inner space of consciousness is through, around and over the ego. It's about being congruent. Our behavior congruent with our values. As we choose to bring ourselves into congruence we can then begin to experience the expression of that integrity.

In the present reality, that means having the confidence to walk our own path, to stand confidently alone if need be, to defend our spirit without compromise. Exercising integrity is indeed the path of the spiritual warrior.

Openness, respect, integrity these are principles that need to underpin pretty much every decision that you make.
Justin Trudeau

Gratitude

Wear gratitude like a cloak and it will
feed every corner of your life.
Rumi

Last and most relevant to spiritual maturity is the energetic feeling and use of gratitude. No matter where we are on our path, no matter how much work we feel we have yet to do with ourselves, one of the most supportive and expansive practices is that of both feeling and expressing our gratitude for everything.

We get so busy in our lives, so caught up with what is happening next, next, next that we tend to allow only brief periods of time to experience that basic stillness that represents who we truly are. As we emerge more and more as our true selves, we find experiences to remind us to feel grateful for the grace of all life. We feel gratitude for the pleasure of love and life and wholeness and peacefulness.

Allowing ourselves to be grateful for what is in our lives, as well as the beauty that surrounds us at all times, brings with it amazing changes within our mind, our body and our spirit. It is a sensation that clears the mind, brings us back to the present moment and calms our hearts.

The principle of gratitude is one of the basic tenants of the new world, of the New Reality. To be spiritually mature we cultivate gratitude as a spiritual experience and practice it in our daily lives.

Starry Sky Gratitude Exercise

Take a deep breath. Yes, right now. Take a deep breath while you are reading this. Go ahead. Then let it out. Take another deep breath and slowly, again, let it out.

Place your mind in the setting of a starry night, look up into the sky, see all the stars, the planets, see a crescent moon with a beautiful planet hanging off its lower edge. Allow yourself the feeling of connectedness with all that, the cosmos, and bring in your gratitude for those stars, that sky, for the Earth, for the air we breathe; feel gratitude for your beating heart and for all life forms on this planet. Acknowledge the love you feel and know that really All Is Well.

The Vibration of Gratitude

If we allow a wave of gratitude to wash over us right now we feel that wave, that feeling, is something that enhances everything that we wish to accomplish in this world. That may sound odd, as gratitude usually seems to just be about what you think of as a feeling or sensory experience. But gratitude is more than that. Becoming or allowing ourselves to be grateful for what IS brings with it amazing changes within mind, body and spirit. It is a sensation that seems to clear the mind and bring us back to the present moment.

Gratitude is a premise, a foundation, a beginning place for many, many things to come our way. As we venture on our way, we open our hearts to the reality that gratitude is a vibration and the vibration of gratitude extends to all who come in contact with us. As we live the gratitude, as we live this vibration, we can tap into its very nature and it will change the way we act, the way we feel, the way we are and the way others experience us along the way.

Our love has no bounds. It is aligned with our gratitude in ways mostly unfathomable to our human minds. It is stepping out of the mind and moving into the heart that we can feel and be that vibration of gratitude.

In Conclusion

With emotional and spiritual maturity comes the realization that being the REAL you creates a more authentic person, a more authentic way of life. It is about breaking free from limitations and conditions of the past and moving to a more passionate level of living.

Gratitude, warm, sincere, intense, when it takes possession
of the bosom, fills the soul to overflowing and scarce
leaves room for any other sentiment or thought.
John Quincy Adams

The Beginning of the New You, the REAL You!

The snow goose need not bathe to make itself white.
Neither need you do anything but be yourself.
Lao Tzu

Welcome to the final chapter! You made it! Wow, we have been on such an amazing journey since first starting the book. Hopefully you have had a chance to work with The Five Keys and have explored the attributes of emotional and spiritual maturity.

If so, by now you have probably gained valuable insight into your amazing, extraordinary self. You have learned and grown, and have become more emotionally and spiritually mature. I imagine you have made huge strides on the way to becoming the REAL you. Congratulations!

The Rewards of Self-Discovery

The path of self-discovery is filled with rewards beyond measure. It is filled with such an abundance of emotions, thoughts, feelings, opinions, ideas and revelations ... all of which are unique to you.

Becoming the REAL you requires love and commitment. And it does not happen overnight. In truth, it is a lifelong journey. It is ongoing. We are evolving and changing every day.

All of the practices contained within this book require constant vigilance. That monkey mind really wants to assert itself all the time! Our old programming is running on an endless loop and needs to be consciously upgraded over and over again.

Anyone who has ever looked inside knows that the work takes persistence. It takes desire. It takes heart!

The New You Emerging

If you choose to truly dedicate yourself to the work, or if you are already well on your way, you will notice some significant changes beginning to emerge and bloom within you.

Here are some attributes you can expect to see:

You have developed a much stronger connection with yourself, and have become much more aware of how you really feel.

You have become more aware of your own unique conditioning, and may have even taken some steps to release or modify it.

You have become more aware of your monkey mind, and have begun to tame it.

You are able to notice your internal and external dialogue more frequently, and better understand the power of your words.

You have begun to accept yourself more, and are kinder to yourself.

You have detached from the past, becoming much more fully present.

You have recognized the strength of your vulnerability and no longer feel such a strong urge to protect it.

You don't care so much about what others think, as you place a high value on your own inner wisdom and heartfelt opinions.

You are able to forgive yourself and others more easily.

You have developed a more balanced, steady and inner focus.

You have become more trusting of your intuition and take time regularly to quiet your mind and tune in.

You have a much stronger sense of who you really are.

You have become more open and honest, especially with yourself.

Your emotional and spiritual maturity is continuing to blossom as you become more and more confident within yourself.

You have released fears that have kept you stuck.

You have let go of your attachment to the outcome of things.

Your behavior has become more congruent with your values.

You have stepped more fully into the New Reality.

You have stepped more fully into becoming the REAL you!

Being the REAL You

Who you really are is unique, and you can choose to be any way you want to be in this world. The choice is yours.

When we talk about becoming the REAL you, it doesn't mean that we have to become some kind of extrovert, glad handing, public person. It doesn't mean that we have to smile all the time or walk around wearing a white robe being saintly. Nor does it mean that we should only think about ourselves and just do whatever our true self feels like doing. It means that we make conscious choices and decisions about how we want to be in this world, based upon a deeper understanding of who we really are.

Being the REAL you is about waking up and stepping out of your conditioned thought patterns about how you think you should be or ought to be, and stepping more fully into just being your REAL, true, authentic self. No longer hiding or protecting yourself from the possible judgment and criticism that might come from the outside world.

A Way of Life

Being the REAL you is about doing the inner work on a daily basis. It means that each and every day we make a conscious choice to become more authentic, more of who we really are.

As we progress along the path, the inner work becomes a way of life: We notice our thoughts. We pay attention to that monkey mind of ours. We converse with it. We watch our words. We notice when we are not treating ourselves nicely, and we change it up. We catch ourselves if we are being rude or dishonest or judgmental. And from there we seek to understand the reasons, with honesty and compassion. We forgive ourselves and others, daily if necessary. We regularly tune into our feelings. We ask ourselves questions so that we can better understand. We frequently bring ourselves back to the present moment. We regularly tune into our heart, the place where we are most REAL, and we allow that place to guide us.

Doing the inner work to become the REAL you is truly a way of life. It is a new way of being. A more conscious way of being.

I offer my sincere admiration to those who have the courage to do it. I know it takes a great deal of personal dedication to become more REAL every day. To do the inner work necessary to discover the truth of who you really are, and then to live that truth wholeheartedly.

As you continue along the path to becoming the REAL you, it will become more and more apparent how very important and deeply meaningful this journey really is. It is truly a significant adventure ... the evolution of your very own consciousness.

And you, my dear one, are truly extraordinary!

Congratulations and welcome to #thenewyou!

Love and Trust, my dear ones ... Love and Trust!

Self-Discovery
Journal

Self-Discovery Journal

_____

_____

_____

_____

_____

_____

_____

_____

_____

_____

_____

_____

_____

~ Recognizing who you really are
allows you to shine forth in the world. ~

~ Let go of who you think you are.
Get in touch with what matters most to you. ~

~ Becoming the real you comes from the heart. ~

~ Learn how to be who you truly are.
Express it all along the way. ~

~ Trust yourself to go ahead and say what you mean
and mean what you say. ~

~ Fearlessly share your gifts of insight and
perception with others. ~

~ Break free from the limitations and conditionings of the past and move to a more passionate level of living. ~

~ Being nicer to ourselves harmonizes our inner space
and brings us a peaceful co-existence with
our monkey mind and our heart. ~

~ The practice of monitoring our thoughts, exercising self-compassion and observing the way we treat ourselves can change everything. ~

~ Always remember that words have power. That is the reason why the way we talk about ourselves matters. ~

~ Give up your ideas about who you were
and be who you are now. ~

~ Allow yourself to be vulnerable and step out
with your real self hanging out. ~

~ The practice of non-attachment is not so much about what we hold on to as what holds on to us. ~

~ A big part of becoming who we really are is about strengthening the relationship we have with ourselves. ~

~ Trust in yourself no matter what is happening. ~

~ When we stay true to ourselves, even when faced with opinions that are different from our own, we'll gain more confidence in ourselves and in our beliefs. ~

~ Our lives really do reflect how we are treating ourselves. ~

~ When we speak our truth, there is an openness
that comes from our heart that releases us and allows
more and more love and support to come in. ~

~ Our past does not have to define our present.
Our failings do not have to define our future. ~

~ Forgive yourself and love yourself unconditionally. ~

~ Other people's perspective of us, their opinions about how we do or do not do things, is really none of our business. ~

~ Gratitude is a premise, a foundation, a beginning place for many, many things to come our way. ~

~ Integrity is not just about telling the truth. It is not just about being a good person. It is about integrating our values so that we are living in the truth of who we are. ~

~ Acknowledging, learning, trusting and further developing our intuition is a part of grounding and expanding ourselves as we become more real and authentic. ~

~ Every move and every step we take is guided and
supported by our intuition. ~

~ Humility and self-confidence together awaken us to greater, vaster perspectives of who we really are. ~

~ Being authentic is about not pretending anymore and just doing what feels right from the heart. ~

~ Even our smallest thought, word and action has a
real effect throughout the Universe. ~

~ Accept others and recognize the perfection of the
soul and spirit in everyone. ~

~ When we choose to become more open and honest, we give ourselves the opportunity to create a deeper connection with ourselves. ~

_____

_____

_____

_____

_____

_____

_____

_____

_____

_____

_____

_____

_____

_____

~ What we value makes up the essence of who we are. ~

~ The real true self is the one listening to the mind do its thing. ~

~ Forgiveness comes from the heart.
It is something we do to take care of ourselves. ~

~ Losing the past is not about losing the memories. It is really about losing the attachment. Let it all go. ~

~ It is not the rational mind that forgives,
It is the heart. ~

~ Being vulnerable means that we allow ourselves
to be who we are without fear of criticism or judgment. ~

~ Self-forgiveness is a very, very powerful tool of liberation. ~

~ When we shift our focus to being present in the here and now, we can feel deep in our souls that there never was, nor will there ever be, any other experience than the present moment. ~

~ Switch to trusting your heart's knowingness, your heart's wisdom, and not the voice in your head. ~

~ You are your most important relationship. Self to self. ~

~ Becoming more conscious of ourselves makes it possible to reach new levels of understanding. ~

~ It is time to bring forth information from the deepest source of your own personal truth, from your own inner wisdom. ~

~ Never underestimate the beautiful power and freedom that washes over you when you commit to being true to yourself. ~

ABOUT THE AUTHOR

Darity Wesley

Darity Wesley is an award-winning author, lawyer, speaker, Death Diva and Modern Day Oracle. She is an innovator and advocate for conscious dying, becoming your True Self and birthing the New Reality. Darity recently concluded a successful 35-year legal career, and is now focusing full time on writing the *Modern Day Oracle Wisdom Teaching Series*™. Through this series, Darity provides guidance and support to those seeking personal growth and/or spiritual transformation. She brings a perspective that is wise and experienced, having travelled the spiritual, metaphysical, esoteric and personal development path for many decades. Her *Modern Day Oracle*™ publications have been inspiring readers around the world since 2006.

If you would like to join Darity's *Modern Day Oracle*™ community, please visit our website and subscribe!

www.DarityWesley.com

To contact the author, please send an email to
info@DarityWesley.com

NOTES

Opening Page

Cummings, E. E. (1894-1962) American poet

Wait! What??? Aren't I Already ME?

Lao Tzu (6th Century BCE) Ancient Chinese philosopher and author, most notably, the *Tao Te Ching*

Self Discovery

Aristotle (334-322 BCE) Ancient Greek philosopher

Inscription on the Temple of Apollo at Delphi, Ancient Greece, 4th century BCE

Maslow, Abraham (1908-1970) American psychologist, from an article entitled 'A Theory of Human Motivation,' *Psychological Review*, 1943

Tolle, Eckhart "The Core of Ego," and "Finding Who You Truly Are" from A NEW EARTH: AWAKENING TO YOUR LIFE'S PURPOSE by Eckhart Tolle, copyright © 2005 by Eckhart Tolle. Used by permission of Dutton, an imprint of Penguin Publishing Group, a division of Penguin Random House LLC. All rights reserved.

What Is the Monkey Mind and How Do We Tame It?

Rumi (1207-1273) Poet and Sufi mystic

Buddhism and the Monkey Mind. Exact quote: "*Just as a monkey, swinging through a forest wilderness, grabs a branch. Letting go of it, it grabs another branch. Letting go of that, it grabs another one. Letting go of that, it grabs another one. In the same way, what's called 'mind,' 'intellect,' or 'consciousness' by day and by night arises as one thing and ceases as another.*" By Assutavā Sutta, as translated by Thanissaro Bhikkhu.

Twain, Mark (1835-1910) American author, most notably, *Tom Sawyer* and *Adventures of Huckleberry Finn*

Aurelius, Marcus (121-180 AD) Roman Emperor

The New Reality

Solara American author. Creator of the Heart of AN, author of *How to Live Large on a Small Planet, Star-Borne Unlimited*; 1st edition, 1996. ©2018 Solara. All rights reserved. Used with permission. www.nvisible.com

The Five Keys to Unlocking the REAL You

Buddha (6th to 5th century BCE) Buddhist figurehead, specifically Gautama Buddha

Rumi (1207-1273) Poet and Sufi mystic

Key #1 Accept Yourself

Rogers, Carl (1902-1987) American psychologist, among the founders of Humanistic Psychotherapy. Author, most notably, *On Becoming a Person*, 1954

Eadie, Betty J. *Embraced By The Light*, 1992 © 1992 Betty J. Eadie. All rights reserved. Used with permission. www.embracedbythelight.com

O'Mara, Peggy 'A Lantern for Lori,' *Mothering Magazine*, Issue Number 128, January-February 2005, pages 8-12. © Peggy O'Mara. All rights reserved. Used with permission.

Martin, George R.R. *A Song of Ice and Fire*, a series of fantasy novels, the first of which is *A Game of Thrones*. The quote is from the American fantasy drama television series created by David Benioff and D. B. Weiss, *Game of Thrones*, Season 7, Episode 1: Dragonstone

Johnson, Wendell (1906-1965) American psychologist, actor and author. Author of *Because I Stutter*, D. Appleton and Company, © 1930 Wendell Johnson

Yoda, The Jedi Master Star Wars™ *The Empire Strikes Back*, 1980. LucasFilm, Ltd./The Walt Disney Studios

Kaveney, Dr. Wendy American author, most notably, *Me and My Senses* © 2016 Wendy Kaveney. Founder and Director of Operations for SOUL: School of Universal Learning charter school. All rights reserved. Used with permission. www.soulcharterschool.org

Key #2 Lose the Past

Buddha (6th to 5th century BCE) Buddhist figurehead, specifically Gautama Buddha

Coffin, Ingrid Creator of *Meta-Thoughts*: Original quotes and concepts designed to take you beyond your habitual thought patterns. © 2015 Ingrid Coffin. All rights reserved. Used with permission. www.IngridCoffin.com

Socrates (470-399 BC) Ancient Greek philosopher. Quote taken from Plato's *The Apology of Socrates, 399 BCE: 'If, as Socrates said, the unexamined life is not worth living ...'*

Hesse, Hermann (1877-1962) German poet. Author of the classic novel *Siddhartha*, 1922

Seabury, David *The Art of Selfishness: How To Deal With the Tyrants and the Tyrannies in Your Life*, Garden City Pub. Co., 1937

Chopra, Dr. Deepak Indian-born American author, public speaker, alternative medicine advocate, and more. Notable author of *Ageless Body, Timeless Mind*, © 1993 Deepak Chopra, M.D. www.DeepakChopra.com www.Chopra.com

Key #3 Allow Yourself to Be Vulnerable

Brown, Brené Research professor at the University of Houston, Houston, Texas. Author of, most notably, *Daring Greatly: How the Courage to Be Vulnerable Transforms the Way We Live, Love, Parent, and Lead*, [New York]: Penguin Random House, ©2012 Brené Brown. All rights reserved. Used with permission. www.BreneBrown.com

Buddha (6th to 5th century BCE) Buddhist figurehead, specifically Gautama Buddha

Dreaver, Jim *The Guardian* magazine, August 2013 (Jiddu Krishnamurti story)

Key #4 Stop Caring What Others Think

Hubbard, Elbert (1856-1915) American writer, artist and philosopher. Author of, most notably, *Little Journeys to the Homes of the Great*, 1910

Lao Tzu (6th Century BCE) Ancient Chinese philosopher and author, most notably, the *Tao Te Ching*

Feynman, Richard (1918-1988) American physicist. He expanded the understanding of quantum electrodynamics, translated Mayan hieroglyphics and cut to the heart of the Challenger disaster. www.feynman.com

Ruiz, Dr. Don Miguel Mexican author of Toltec spiritualist and neoshamanistic texts. From the book *The Four Agreements* © 1997 Miguel Angel Ruiz, M.D. Reprinted by permission of Amber-Allen Publishing, Inc. San Rafael, CA. All rights reserved. www.amberallen.com www.miguelruiz.com

Dass, Ram American teacher, author and clinical psychologist. *Be Here Now*, Lama Foundation, [San Cristobal, New Mexico], 1971 © 1971 Ram Dass. All rights reserved. www.RamDass.org

Geisel, Theodor Seuss "Ted" (1904-1991) American author and poet known as Dr. Seuss. According to our research, there is no substantive evidence that Dr. Seuss made this remark. It does not show up in any of his printed material. It was attributed to him in the 2000s as a popular saying in school yearbooks. The earliest instance of this saying found in print was placed between quotation marks signaling that it was probably an anonymous piece of wisdom in 1938, in the *Journal of the Institution of Municipal and County Engineers*. www.seussville.com

Key #5 Be Open and Honest

Joosab, Fathima Bibi Author of, most notably, *Inspirations of the Heart: Sister Fathima's Open Heart*, 2017

Anderson, Walter (1885-1962) German author and folklorist

Freud, Sigmund (1856-1939) Austrian neurologist, founder of psychoanalysis. Author of most notably, *The Interpretation of Dreams* 1899. Translated from German to English by MacMillian Publishing, 1913

Moynihan, Daniel Patrick "Pat" (1924-2003) American politician

Reference regarding biblical admonition (about *picking the speck of sawdust in someone else's eye while paying no attention to the plank in your own eye.*) Matthew 7:3, (New International Version)

King, Jr., Martin Luther (1929-1968) American Baptist minister and activist. Most noted for his "I Have a Dream" public speech delivered during the *March on Washington for Jobs and Freedom* on August 28, 1963 www.thekingcenter.org

Reference regarding biblical admonition (about Jesus saying on the cross, *Father, forgive them, for they don't know what they are doing.*) Luke 23:34 (New International Version)

In Conclusion: The Five Keys to Unlocking the REAL You

Dickens, Charles (1812-1870) English writer. Author of, most notably, *A Christmas Carol*, 1843 and *Oliver Twist*, 1838

Emotional Maturity

Kornfield, Jack American author, most notably, *A Path With Heart*, 1993 www.jackkornfield.com

Goleman, Daniel American author, most notably, *Emotional intelligence: Why it can matter more than IQ*, Bantam Books, 1995 www.danielgoleman.info

Salovey, Peter and Mayer, John Authors of *Emotional Intelligence: Imagination, Cognition and Personality*, article published 1990. Although Salovey and Mayer are credited with coining the term 'Emotional Intelligence', they attribute it to earlier researchers such as Wayne Payne.

Responsibility

Covey, Stephen R. (1932-2012) American educator, author and businessman. *The 7 Habits of Highly Successful People: Powerful Lessons in Personal Change*, 1989, Free Press. Updated ©2015 Franklin Covey Co.

Freud, Sigmund (1856-1939) Austrian neurologist, founder of psychoanalysis. Author of most notably, *The Interpretation of Dreams* 1899. Translated from German to English by MacMillian Publishing, 1913

His Holiness the Dalai Lama, Tibetan spiritual leader, specifically Tenzin Gyatso, 14th Dalai Lama. Author of, most notably, *The Art of Happiness* 1998 © 1998 HH Dali Lama and Howard C. Cutler, MD www.dalailama.com

Flexibility

Gandhi, Mahatma (1869-1948) Indian activist and civil rights leader.

Dooley, Mike New York Times bestselling author, speaker, and entrepreneur in the philosophical New Thought movement. ©Mike Dooley, www.tut.com

Gladwell, Malcolm Canadian author, most notably *Blink: The Power of Thinking Without Thinking,* as quoted during a live interview with Paul Holdengräber at the New York Public Library's *LIVE from the NYPL* series, April 1, 2014

Einstein, Albert (1879-1955) German physicist

Non-Judgment

Krishnamurti, Jiddu (1895-1986) Indian philosopher

Rana, Pushpa Indian author, most notably, *Just The Way I Feel*

Roosevelt, Theodore (1858-1919) American statesman and writer, 26th President of the United States

Associates for Personal and Family Counseling, *Characteristics of Emotional Maturity*, San Diego, 1990

Spiritual Maturity

Hawkins, M.D., Ph.D., David R. *I: Reality and Subjectivity*, 2003, Chapter 6, *Realization*, pg. 173. Used with permission of Veritas Publishing. ©2003 David R. Hawkins. All rights reserved. www.Veritaspub.com

Pearce, Susan Bliss American author. From the book *OM-LESS? An Irreverent Guide to Knowing Grace*, page 101, Intellect Publishing, ©2016 Susan Bliss Pearce. All rights reserved. Used with permission.

Non-Attachment

Buddha (6th to 5th century BCE) Buddhist figurehead, specifically Gautama Buddha

His Holiness the Dalai Lama, Tibetan spiritual leader, specifically Tenzin Gyatso, 14th Dalai Lama. Author of, most notably, *The Art of Happiness* 1998 © 1998 HH Dali Lama and Howard C. Cutler, MD www.dalailama.com

Compassion and Tolerance

His Holiness the Dalai Lama, Tibetan spiritual leader, specifically Tenzin Gyatso, 14th Dalai Lama. Author of, most notably, *The Art of Happiness* 1998 © 1998 HH Dali Lama and Howard C. Cutler, MD www.dalailama.com

Keltner, Dacher Professor of Psychology at the University of California, Berkeley. From essay *The Compassionate Instinct*, 2004 greatergood.berkeley.edu

Introspection

Aristotle (334-322 BCE) Ancient Greek philosopher

Tolle, Eckhart "The Core of Ego," and "Finding Who You Truly Are" from A NEW EARTH: AWAKENING TO YOUR LIFE'S PURPOSE by Eckhart Tolle, copyright © 2005 by Eckhart Tolle. Used by permission of Dutton, an imprint of Penguin Publishing Group, a division of Penguin Random House LLC. All rights reserved.

Intuition

Yogananda, Paramahansa (1893-1952) Indian yogi and author, from article *How to Develop Your Intuition,* 1939

Authenticity

Smith, Cristina American author, Yoga for the Brain™ Series, from *The Word Search Sage,* page 105 © 2017 Cristina Smith. Published by Sudoku Wisdom. All rights reserved. Used with permission. www.sudokuwisdom.com www.CristinaSmith.com

Tolle, Eckhart "The Core of Ego," and "Finding Who You Truly Are" from A NEW EARTH: AWAKENING TO YOUR LIFE'S PURPOSE by Eckhart Tolle, copyright © 2005 by Eckhart Tolle. Used by permission of Dutton, an imprint of Penguin Publishing Group, a division of Penguin Random House LLC. All rights reserved.

Integrity

Brown, Brené Research professor at the University of Houston, Texas. Author of, most notably, *Daring Greatly: How the Courage to Be Vulnerable Transforms the Way We Live, Love, Parent, and Lead,* [New York]: Penguin Random House, ©2012 Brené Brown. All rights reserved. Used with permission. www.BreneBrown.com

Trudeau, Justin PC, MP Canadian politician, 23rd Prime Minister of Canada since 2015 and Leader of the Liberal Party since 2013

Gratitude

Rumi (1207-1273) Poet and Sufi mystic

Adams, John Quincy (1767-1848) American statesman, the 6th President of the United States

The Beginning of the New You, the REAL You!

Lao Tzu (6th Century BCE) Ancient Chinese philosopher and author, most notably, the *Tao Te Ching*

***

All unattributed quotes are ©2006-2018 Darity Wesley
All rights reserved.

GRATITUDE AND APPRECIATION

The creation of this book, my second in the *Wisdom Teaching Series*, has been such a wonderful flow of love and energy. So many folks participated and supported me in various parts of its formation. I thank each and every one of them for their generosity and kindness!

To my tireless absolutely amazing and awesome assistant and Graphic Designer, Paula Wansley, I give my thanks, appreciation and gratitude. Her creative brilliance in the design of the covers, the five keys, all the graphics and layout truly enhance the overall quality of the book, making the ambiance clear, calm and easy. Her contributing expertise and perspectives on the entire work, helped make *How To Be the REAL You* a more dynamic tool for exploring and discovering who you really are. In addition, her care and encouragement of me, personally, and of the entire publishing process has been phenomenal. I am so very grateful, from the bottom of my heart, for all of her help.

To my extraordinarily excellent and exceptional editor, Melissa Morgan, my heart pours over with thanks and gratitude. Melissa has helped me stay on the straight and narrow, has helped with clarity, grammar, concepts and ideas where necessary, time after time. Her editorial expertise has kept me grammatically safe and sound. I am so appreciative for all she has done to support the creation of this series. She is an astoundingly capable woman and I appreciate her.

To all my fantastically fabulous friends who provided feedback on various portions of the work, thank you.

To my writing sister and forever friend, Cristina Smith who proofed the final copy and supports me every step of the way, much love and thanks to you!

And a very special thanks to my husband, Robert, who continues to stand by me and support me and my dreams. He has really been after me for years to do this work. His love continues to keep me steady on the beam. I certainly would not be the person I am today without him. My heart expands because of his belief in me and his love. He really gives me lots of opportunities to be the REAL me. Thanks, honey!

Modern Day

ORACLE™

You Can Transform Your Life

Modern Day Oracle™ Wisdom Teaching Series
Book 1

How To Be the REAL You

Modern Day Oracle™ Wisdom Teaching Series
Book 2

Modern Day Oracle™ Wisdom Teaching Series

How To Be the REAL You
Go Deeper
Workbook

Darity Wesley
Melissa Morgan
Paula Wansley

How To Be
the REAL You

Go Deeper

Companion Workbook for
How To Be the REAL You
by Darity Wesley

Provides a more in-depth exploration of the
How To Be the REAL You process

Go Deeper contains ...

- Supplemental self-discovery questions to promote
deeper introspection and higher levels of awareness.

- Bonus exercises and information to help identify and
break free from old patterns of conditioning.

- Practical advice for working more closely with
The Five Keys to Becoming the REAL You.

**For those seeking to *go deeper* on their
journey of self-discovery and to
become who they really are!**

ISBN 978-0-9995425-3-8

Award winning best seller!

Modern Day Oracle™ Wisdom Teaching Series

You Can Transform Your Life

Darity Wesley

Winner 2017 New Apple Literary Award

*Solo Medalist Winner
Inspirational/ Motivational/Self-Help*

YOU CAN TRANSFORM YOUR LIFE

by Darity Wesley

Have you ever dreamed of making changes to your life ...
to feel more in harmony with yourself and your world?

Have you ever wished you could express your true potential ...
to live a life that expresses who you really are?

Have you ever wanted to increase your intuition ...
to communicate with your Higher Self, Guides and Angels?

If so, You Can Transform Your Life provides a way!

You Can Transform Your Life provides processes, tools and practices to take you on a journey of transformation. Offers a simple step-by-step plan to support you every step of the way!

Contains 52 Oracle messages of inspiration, affirmation mantras and symbols, with many practical tips and tools for deep inner transformation, leading you along the path of self-discovery and to new levels of awareness.

You Can Transform Your Life provides a plan that can help support and guide you on a journey of personal growth and spiritual transformation.

Modern Day

ORACLE

Modern Day Oracle™ Wisdom Teaching Series Book 1

Modern Day Oracle™ Wisdom Teaching Series

You Can Transform Your Life

Go Deeper

Workbook

Darity Wesley
Melissa Morgan
Paula Wansley

You Can Transform Your Life

Go Deeper

Companion Workbook for
You Can Transform Your Life
by Darity Wesley

Provides a more in-depth exploration of the
You Can Transform Your Life process

Go Deeper contains ...

- Additional questions for each of the 52 Oracle Messages
to promote deeper self-discovery and awareness.

- Bonus exercises and information to help increase
intuition, spiritual strength and inner balance.

- Practical advice on how to apply *Modern Day Oracle™*
tools of transformation to all areas of your life.

For those seeking to *go deeper* on their
journey of transformation!

ISBN 978-0-9995425-1-4

PRAISE FOR DARITY'S BOOK
You Can Transform Your Life

Winner 2017 New Apple Literary Award
Solo Medalist Winner
Inspirational/ Motivational/Self-Help

Darity's insights and writings will have you captured. She has a fresh and engaging perspective and her teachings are amazing. *Karen*

I'm looking forward to diving into my inner voice while being guided by a voice of wisdom, peace and love! Darity shares with us messages on true happiness from within! Thank you, Thank you, Thank you!
- Shannon

This book is AH-mazing! It challenges you to think deeper about your life, but in a supportive and insightful way. This book is SO easy to use! *Lindsay Nakagawa, San Diego, CA*

I absolutely love, love, love this book! Darity has written such a good guide for helping us to live wonderful lives and to help us learn how to survive what is happening in this world now. Both my husband and I really appreciate how the format of the book is so easy to read and understand. I love that each Oracle is written from the heart—so much common sense and yet such help in how to live and how to be our true selves. Her positive words and wisdom really do enforce what we know is right. It gives us the strength we need to understand the love that is there for us always. *Lynn Woehrle, Newman Lake, WA*

I love the journey this book, **You Can Transform Your Life,** takes you on and how it inspires me each day. The author does a very good job at making the material interactive and easily digestible so that the messages really sink in. It's like having a life coach right beside me every morning motivating me to keep striving for the things that matter most and letting go of the things that don't serve me. I can't wait for her next book! I hope it is coming with another workbook. I found that really valuable last time, and it also allowed me to stretch the book out longer, since I didn't want it to end! ☺ *Sarah Burchard, Honolulu, Hawaii*

I have been very fortunate to have the honor of reading Darity's writings for years. She knows what needs to be said, and knows how to communicate it clearly. She is willing to share her wisdom and the beauty of her heart to whomever wants to hear. The book, **You Can Transform Your Life,** can do just that! *Janni, Millwood, WA*

Darity is praise and prayer to lips of gathering minds, hearts and souls whom ALL share her wisdom. A wisdom so fundamental in truth that it is recognizable to the heart of mankind, ALL that is. *J. Lewis*

I love that I can easily jump into this *journey* in a way that works for me. It is written and structured in a way that meets my needs for being able to start making changes right now, (I began the first day I picked up the book!) and then being able to go at my own pace. I also appreciate that the author encourages *guidance coming from within ourselves* rather than only the Oracle messages and affirmation mantras provided. Lastly, I highly recommend any book that both creates self-reflection in addition to filling me with hope, love, and joy! *Alannah*

The **You Can Transform Your Life** book and workbook is inspiring and interesting. Thought provoking and insightful. It has given me yet another springboard into personal growth and change. I see new doors and windows opening up for me. You'd think by now, at age 72, that all my ducks would be neatly in a row. But I have learned that each passing stage in life opens doors for learning and growing. Reading this material and, just as important, writing down my reflections, has indeed supported my efforts to "Be the best me at 73!" So, regardless of your age or place in this life, there is a good time to pick up **You Can Transform Your Life** and consider the yet untapped potential in your life! *Jayne Chelberg-Sams, El Cajon, CA*

Editorial Reviews

Imagine if you could have a year of inspiration mapped out for you. Well, Darity Wesley has done just that. **You Can Transform Your Life** was written as a guide to support your personal and spiritual growth over the course of 52 weeks. I found that answering the featured questions and using the space provided to journal my emotions and thoughts on the Oracle message made it so much more powerful. I think you will be amazed at how far you've come on your personal journey by the time you reach the last journal page, which prompts, *Free yourself from what is holding you back! Be who you truly are! Becca Chopra, Becca's Inspirational Book Blog*

You Can Transform Your Life by Darity Wesley is a book filled with insight and wisdom. Using words of strength, and words that unleash creativity in readers, the author ushers them into the realm of endless possibilities where they learn to create the life they really want. The format of the book makes it a very easy tool for readers to use, with spaces for personal notes, mantras and affirmations that will help readers stay focused, lift their spirits, and help them stay committed to their course. **You Can Transform Your Life** is an empowering book for readers who want to step up their growth game and rise above mediocrity, a sure path to success! *Divine Zape, Readers' Favorite*

There are lots of *transform your life* type books in the marketplace, yet, Darity Wesley's **You Can Transform Your Life** rises above the rest. It provides unique insights and thought provoking interactivity. She encourages you to use your personal intuition in addition to the wisdom of her Oracles. This leads to the transformation of living your best, most authentic life. *Brenda Krueger Huffman, Publisher, Women's Voices Magazine*

Best Book Winner
2017 Pinnacle Achievement Award
Games and Puzzles

THE WORD SEARCH ORACLE

Yoga for the Brain™

Featuring Modern Day Oracle™ messages by Darity Wesley!

Every puzzle is both a challenge to be solved and a meditation for self-realization.

Filled with fascinating facts and enlightening insights.

Enjoy 60 fun-filled word search puzzles each with a hidden Oracle message!

Have fun with a purpose!

The Word Search Oracle Invites You to Play!

ISBN 978-1544211558